The
RETROSEXUAL
MANUAL

AUTHOR'S DEDICATION:
For Mary and Mala – who have never got in the way of
a man, his pint and his football.

Published in Great Britain in 2008 by
Prion
An imprint of the
Carlton Publishing Group
20 Mortimer Street
London W1T 3JW

10 9 8 7 6 5 4 3 2 1

A catalogue record for this book is available from the British Library

ISBN 978-1-85375-656-6

Printed and bound in Great Britain by Mackays of Chatham Ltd

The
RETROSEXUAL
MANUAL

How to be a real man

Dave Besley

PRION

CONTENTS

INTRODUCTION: WHERE DID ALL THE MEN GO?

They've been neutering cats and dogs for centuries; it makes them safer, more loveable and less likely to roam. Fortunately, they only got round to neutering men in the last 20-odd years in a bid to create a tame, timid, asexual creature barely worthy of the name. Otherwise there'd have been no Cromwell or Mandela, no Shakespeare or Hemingway, not even a Best or a Bowles.

Somehow, as feminism, gay rights and smarmy marketing execs were embraced by the late 20th century, man's identity was stolen from under our noses.

They've taken away our language, our clothes, our pubs, our cars, even our confidence – our very essence of manliness. They couldn't have castrated us more effectively if they'd clapped a pair of bricks around our knackers.

Like some scary science fiction movie, there are a few who escaped; who still manage to live a full life as real men. But there are many more who feel the pain, as if they'd been castrated only yesterday. These are the ranks who are determined to reclaim their balls – and scratch them regularly to make sure they're still there. These are the Retrosexuals.

And who are their biggest allies in this great fightback? Women. By an incredible stroke of luck, at the same time as men are feeling emasculated, strangled, frustrated and like they're really not getting enough sex, women are becoming impatient with the pathetic, wet, blubbing fops that pass for blokes in the 21st century. Modern women yearn for a man who answers back; who offers challenge or danger; a man who will look them in the eye and tell them to shut up when their neurotic whining has become too much; a man whose very lifestyle shouts drama, risk and, above all, sex.

Ah, but you're not that man, are you? You're too worried about upsetting someone, about breaking a social taboo or appearing a little brusque. You're still thinking you'll get in her knickers by trudging round the shopping mall all day and sitting on leather couches in bars with big mirrors drinking oh-so-amusingly-rude-named cocktails.

This book is the key to unlock your chains: the inspiration you need to walk tall, unleash your true manhood on the world and get the girl. You won't find it easy; there's a lot you're going to have to unlearn and some traits you'll have to dig way down in your soul to reclaim. Are you man enough for the job? If you've bought this book, you're already on your way. If you're just browsing, then make your bloody mind up – and let that be lesson one!

1. WIMP NATION

'Ben embodies a new generation of men who show their strength in their personality but are not afraid to care for their appearance,' a L'Oreal spokesperson spewed out to *Hello!* magazine after the company appointed effete movie actor Ben Affleck as its representative.

What a brave new world this is, where men may be afraid of speaking out of turn, scared shitless of expressing opinions, terrified of actually acting like men... but, thank heavens, 'not afraid to care for their appearance'. Welcome to Wimp Nation.

In 1966, as Bobby Moore approached the Queen in order to receive the World Cup trophy, he quickly wiped his hand down his shirt. It wouldn't have been right to soil Her Majesty's white gloves with some bought-and-paid-for gland juice. More than 30 years later – in the same tournament – as England left the field after an uninspiring defeat by Brazil, the South Americans' match-winner Ronaldinho remarked how the shirt he'd swapped with David Beckham had such a strong whiff of perfume that he couldn't even smell the sweat. This has been the descent of man over those 30 years: from proud, hard-working bloke to sad, self-obsessed fop.

For the 1970s man, confidence was everything; he did what he did because he knew it was right. But once he had that knocked out of him by an accumulation of political events (such as the rise of feminism, the worship of 'marketing' and the destruction of the manufacturing industries) he was left lying in the gutter, legs akimbo, ready for anyone who fancied giving him a good kick in the knackers. Suddenly this Neanderthal, unreconstructed, sexist pig was unfashionable, a source of humour and not fit for purpose.

The modern man was sensitive, in touch with his emotions and ready to spend his days tippy-toeing over eggshells in order to avoid upsetting anyone. And they built a society around him – full of health and safety regulations, parking wardens and ambulance-chasing lawyers. It was no longer enough to be strong and silent; every wet boy with a pair of rimless glasses felt required to pontificate at length about nothing in particular as long as it didn't upset anyone.

It took an Australian, Mark Latham, the former leader of their Labour Party (and a man who once broke a cabbie's arm in a fight over the fare), to spell it out: 'Australian mates and good blokes have been replaced by nervous wrecks, metrosexual knobs and toss bags,' he wrote. 'Instead of calling a spade a spade, our national conversation is now dominated by weasel words and the pretence of politeness.'

METROSEXUAL – NOT SHAGGING ON THE TUBE

The term 'metrosexual' was first coined in 1994 by journalist Mark Simpson. In those, the dog days of Thatcherism, when yuppies and wealth creators were still the tired buzzwords of the day, no one took much notice of his masterly analysis. It wasn't until eight years later, when he returned to the idea, that people finally looked about and thought, 'Yes – that's the berk they've made my new boss.'

Simpson wrote of how the old-fashioned normal bloke had infuriated the efforts of consumer capitalism; how the big problem was that men didn't shop enough. If only a new kind of man could be engineered; a man who was less confident about his identity and more concerned with his image; a man Simpson describes as 'an advertiser's walking wet dream'.

There was nothing more sophisticated, caring or 21st-century about this great evolution; it was just a ruse to get men into shops. But thousands – unable to purchase a giant badge saying, 'I'm a gullible prat' – chose to ignore his criticism and adopt the philosophy and lifestyle of the metrosexual with gusto. Soon, right across the western world, an infant cult which should have been weighted down with rocks, wrapped in a black bin liner and thrown in the canal, was booming.

New York author Michael Flocker brought out *The Metrosexual Guide to Style*, a bible for those who could tear themselves away from the mirror long enough to read. This 'handbook for the modern man' defined the metrosexual as follows: '1: 21st-century male trendsetter. 2: straight, urban man with a heightened aesthetic sense. 3: man who spends time and money on appearance and shopping. 4: man willing to embrace his feminine side.' This new breed seemed chic, sophisticated and unthreatening. Who wouldn't want to join their club? Especially when – it soon became apparent – you were virtually guaranteed sex.

Women, of course, embraced this movement like a free gift from Littlewoods. With no effort on their part, these Barbies had their own little Kens to play with. They could dress them, go out shopping together and watch endless celebrity and reality shows. Now they could all have the gay best friend they had always dreamed of – with the added advantage of having sex (only when they felt like it; no self-regarding metrosexual would dream of trying it on as it was now the ladies' turn to make the first move).

Soon the metrosexual was being joined by other groups keen to muscle in on the more-fashionable-than-thou market. Along came New Man, a touchy, feely sort who didn't go to football; Millennium Man, a kind of let's-define-maleness-again as if the last 100,000 years had never happened type (yeah, right); and Just Gay Enough – enough for what, they don't say – to buy a ticket to see *West Side Story* or to get rogered in the back of an articulated lorry in the Heston service station truck park?

POST-METROSEXUAL – WILL IT NEVER END?

The problem was that some men are just plain ugly and boorish. No amount of lotions, potions and support groups can give them that girlish complexion the PR boys decided was so darned attractive. And so it began all over again. You don't want to bend it like Beckham, you need to be a heteropolitan (so different from metrosexual – see what they've done there?) said the oh-so-influential *Men's Health* magazine, while top advertising executive Marian Salzman coined the term übersexual, 'a new brand of male who mixes strength and confidence with a willingness to communicate and co-operate'. 'Ooh, ooh, let me be one of them; they sound great and maybe this time I'll get laid,' we were expected to chant.

Meanwhile, women were beginning to tire of the results. How had they landed up with men with the maleness taken out, a whole gender of spineless creeps? Well, it was a long story...

Are You A Metrosexual?
10 Tell-Tale Signs That You've Become One Of Them

- You find gay men come on to you and feel flattered.
- You use a conditioner or moisturizer.
- You carry a manbag (that's a purse to you and me) and your suitcase, however small, has wheels.
- You know what colour socks you're wearing.
- You know what a manicure, pedicure, facial or exfoliation is.
- You like to go 'commando'.
- You call men's toiletries 'products'.
- You shave any part of your body except your face or head.
- You know your hairdresser's name.
- You borrow toiletries or clothes from your girlfriend.

THE HISTORY OF MEN AND WOMEN

The name retrosexual implies that we're looking to the past to model our behaviour and attitudes, but the past is a big book and the relationships between men and women have ebbed and flowed over many generations. What lessons can we learn from the past? Were things ever actually 'better'? And have men always been moaned at for not putting the toilet seat down?

Prehistoric Relationships

Food and sex were the major preoccupations of early man (and most were agreed that the food could generally wait). The menfolk of any camp had a small number of essential tasks, namely making the fire, going out hunting, and finding things which made a noise when you banged them. Any spare time they might have had was spent digesting and enjoying hallucinogenics or trying to imagine how a wheel might work. With language still at an early level, discussions were minimal and would consist of a few grunts punctuated by the odd snort. Melvyn Bragg they definitely were not.

The job of the women was to look after the cave and amble out to pick a few berries if the weather was clement. Most of the day was spent shelling peas and nuts, and fine-tuning sewing skills along with the other women of the camp. They were therefore able to develop much more sophisticated conversational skills and use them to discuss the latest in cooking utensils, or how next door's cave wall paintings were *so* Paleolithic.

A woman's expectations of a man were simple; bring me back something decent to eat and please God (or Odin or Thor or whoever) don't let him ejaculate over my best mammoth loincloth again. His conversational skills, or even his looks, were not highly significant. She wanted the alpha male who was most likely to bring home the bacon. Pretty boys were more likely to hear, 'I do like the angle of your cheekbones, but you're the one who's always left with the boar's arse.'

This was man at his most basic. He slept in his clothes, went out to work with his mates, and got dinner and a shag when he wanted. He didn't have to sit around for ages discussing what colour the cave walls might be (even if she was tiring of the sandstone look and wanted a rich mahogany); he wasn't required to make a sauce for the veal escalope (off the bone was just fine); and the only thing he put on his face was a smear of charcoal warpaint when he was off for a bit of local pillaging.

The Dark Ages

By the time tribes had settled into homesteads and farming had developed, life began to get more difficult for Joe Salt-of-the-Earth. He was now expected to wear clothes, although still under little pressure to co-ordinate ('That yokel smock really doesn't match your string belt, Ebenezer'), and working in the fields was so tough he was often too knackered for sex. Worst of all was this new concept of 'church'. No longer was Sunday – his day for getting up late, getting a hundred or so lads together for a football match (now known as a 'brawl') against the next village and getting completely hammered – a day of rest. Now he had to troop off twice a day for hours of repenting and worshipping and generally bemoaning how unworthy he was – in decent clothes. For the first time in history, people were looking at men and judging how they dressed. If the squire's son Julian sported a fine new pair of corduroy breeches, it could dominate the village gossip for a good few years.

And yet there was an upside: the birth of the pub. As women began to make a home the clean, sanitized dwelling it is today, men naturally looked to spend their time somewhere dirty and smelly, where they could feel more at ease. And they served the newfangled 'beer', too – what a bonus! These cramped rooms filled with barrels of something resembling ditch-water soon became a natural refuge for the menfolk – and so they would remain for hundreds of years, until some fool came up with the idea of All Bar One.

Hard times though they were, the Dark Ages represented an equilibrium between men and women that has rarely been matched since. They toiled together in the fields, often drank themselves into a stupor together and happily raised families together, a kind of medieval version of Richard and Judy. A woman's idea of a good catch was a bloke who still had all his limbs intact, didn't smell like he'd bathed in the toilet ditch and managed to get locked in the stocks when her mother was visiting. These were high standards to expect most men to maintain, but the bar was soon to be raised, and man was certain to be on to a loser.

The Renaissance

The flowering of culture from the 14th to the 17th centuries has been described as a watershed for European civilization, but for many men across the continent it was a complete pisser. Having just survived the Black Death – which, admittedly, started out as a good excuse for a couple of sick days off work and progressed to a nice opportunity to stay in bed for a week or two before tailing off into a nasty expiry – the last thing most working

Joes wanted was a blossoming of the spheres of philosophy, art, science, literature and religion.

The Renaissance was mainly driven by monks and academics – people not really in need of a skinful and a good shag of a Friday night – and led to two ideas that would be the curse of men for the centuries that followed: thinking and dating.

Man had survived perfectly well for thousands of years without 'thinking', but suddenly a pleasant evening's belching and farting in the pub was ruined by some herbert wanting to discuss 'the need for realism and human emotion in art'. You could be asked to step outside by a group of thugs eager to show how a mechanical philosophy had replaced the Aristotelian idea of 'final cause', and when your girl interrupted an engrossing bout of rough sex in the local barn with 'What are you thinking?' she was expecting a revealing insight into the nature of human consciousness rather than the relative merits of taking her from behind.

Until now, it was commonly accepted that a relationship was purely built on sex, food and something to cling to in order to keep the hypothermia to a minimum. Women had low expectations and were rarely disappointed. If they'd had them, personal ads might have read: 'Man wanted (preferably without last week's dinner still stuck between his teeth) for a miserable lifelong relationship, regular drunken physical abuse and 20 years of drudgery mothering your village idiot brood.' But all this was about to change as some dreamy idiots on a 15th-century version of a gap year – visiting foreign cities, getting embarrassingly drunk, writing poetry and shoving over-packed rucksacks into the ribs of ordinary folk trying to get to work – invented romantic love.

Wouldn't it be great, they thought, if men had somehow to earn the right to get their end away – and they didn't just mean wiping their boots on the mat or even taking them off. They invented a world where men should worship the beauty of women (even though most women of the time were bald and toothless), become infatuated and willing to do anything for them and present themselves as attractive and interesting specimens – and that was before they even got a good feel.

From this point on, men were doomed. The balance of power had been conceded. Women now realized they had a choice; they didn't have to accept the first oaf who'd won them in a card game with their brother. It would be a rocky downhill road for men from now on – one that would inevitably lead to the hell of long walks in the country and fireside cuddles.

Fops and Frigidity – Elizabethans, Victorians and Lesbians

So it came about that one man would make the next few hundred years bearable for the increasingly hen-pecked, sexually starved man; step forward Sir Walter Raleigh. In introducing the potato – and hence the chip – and tobacco to western civilization, Raleigh gave modern man two of his pillars of life (the third, alcohol, was well established). With chips, beer and fags, men would be able to withstand anything the world could throw at them. And, at his execution, Raleigh himself proved an early retrosexual hero. Not for him the whimperings of the coward or the self-obsession of the diarrhoea-mouthed speechmakers; his last words, as he lay ready for the axe to fall, were: 'Strike, man; strike!'

Meanwhile, the fop had been born. The New Romantics of their day, these straight men began to put on make-up, wigs, frills and tight trousers that displayed their codpieces to the full. No wonder the Spanish thought we were ripe for invasion. And if it hadn't been for old Walter and his mates, the fops would have had plenty of chance to practise the ridiculous lisp they'd pretentiously adopted. On the plus side, we'd have been spared Jamie Oliver discovering 'pukka' olives and a 'delish' *arroz negra*. But another low had been reached; man was now ready to compete with his woman for time in front of the mirror.

Next came the Victorians – the great moral enforcers. Sex had always been the great escape, available to even the poorest sod, but now a miserable bunch of Christian impotents decided it was far too enjoyable to let everybody at it. Obviously the same didn't apply to the Queen Empress. She was happy with Prince Albert wearing his Prince Albert (a penis-piercing believed to enhance sexual enjoyment), but, up and down the land, men had their conjugal rights removed on the grounds that the Lord was watching (a kind of celestial dogging), it would ruin the shape of her bustle and she had to get up at 4.30am to clock in at the mill.

The 1900s were certainly a time when man got his dick caught in the zipper of the zeitgeist. While the period condemned him to rare sexual forays and, even then, was strictly limited to the missionary position, unbridled sex did seem fine, however, between women. Lesbianism flourished, as women explored their sexuality for the first time and discovered it could somehow be a whole lot more fun doing it with a sensual, smooth-skinned girl than some brute with two minutes to spare before the pub opened. Women had realized that if they were clever, men could be reduced to clones whose only use was to bring home some money and carve the Sunday roast. And men had realized they could be excluded from sex altogether – and not even allowed to watch. Little surprise, then, that professional sport took root in these spartan years.

A World at War – Heroes and Villains

There's nothing like a good war to give a man back his sense of priorities. Tommy Atkins, preparing to go over the top at Ypres after two months of life among the rats and mud of the trenches, barely had time to wonder whether exfoliation might do wonders for the condition of his skin; Jock Mackintosh, chasing Messerschmitts and Heinkels across the skies of Kent, probably didn't give too much thought to whether his pecs filled out his flying jacket adequately or whether he should spend more time at the gym; and did Taffy Jones, swept off his merchant ship on a North Atlantic convoy, bemoan the fact that he'd used his best conditioner on his hair and now it was going to be ruined by seawater?

Apart from the genocide, pointless battles, bombing of civilian populations and the endless bully beef, it was a great era. Men were doing what they do best (next to farting and belching simultaneously): getting the job done and showing what solid guys they could be. With women stoically working the land and factories – albeit grateful to the odd American airman for a pair of nylons here and there – it suddenly seemed this could be a land fit for heroes after all.

Once the rationing was over, people were allowed to get on with never having it so good. Rock 'n' roll, television, washing machines, Arthur Askey: they must have had a ball. This was the golden age of the movies, when Hollywood's stars provided the glamour and role models for ordinary people. The sultry delights of Rita Hayworth and pin-up Betty Paige preoccupied men's minds, as they adopted the macho spirit of the likes of Gary Cooper and John Wayne (whose tombstone read 'Feo, Fuerte y Formal,' a Spanish epitaph meaning 'Ugly, strong and dignified' – a retrosexual motto if ever there was one). Meanwhile, as women dreamed of having the looks of an Audrey Hepburn and the homely charm of Doris Day, they wanted their man to be like Rock Hudson (subsequently revealed to be gay), Tab Hunter (who also turned out to be gay) or Troy Donahoe (ditto). Together the two sexes found equilibrium in a dream a million miles away from their humdrum lives.

The 1960s – Free Love at a Cost

OK. It had its downside. Not many men suit that androgynous look, the music was mostly shite, the hippies droned on for ever and ever, but at last – at long last – women were prepared to share their favours liberally (basically a way of saying even ugly blokes got a look in). This, they claimed, was the wonderful dawning of the Age of Aquarius (did no one read the horoscope that mentioned disastrous land wars in Asia, corrupt presidents, Charles Manson and England's defeat by West Germany in the 1970 World Cup?)

when equality, fraternity and liberty would enlighten the planet. For men, it was time to take a few liberties.

In 1961, an earth-shattering development in the relationship between men and women took place – and for those guessing ahead, it wasn't the introduction of Ken, a boyfriend for Barbie. Although initially for married women only, the contraceptive pill had finally been made available. By 1969 more than a million good-time girls were taking it; it would have been a crime not to test out such a medical phenomenon.

For women, the pill was a wrenching apart of the chains which had bound them for so many years, a liberation that was not only sexual but cultural, enabling them to take control of their own lives. For men, it was also a watershed; never before had they enjoyed the chance to shag themselves stupid without responsibility. What marvellous divinity could have devised such a thing? The consequences of the sex act were completely in the hands of the woman; he could wipe up, zip up and walk away without the slightest pang of guilt.

For a few golden years, it looked like it might work. Hippy communities were fuelled by 'free love'; everyone could share in the action as long as they had a kaftan and a droopy moustache. Watching old news footage of the psychedelic festivals, you might be forgiven for believing women spent the latter part of the decade completely topless. This was, of course, a cunning ploy to get soldiers back from Vietnam, but unfortunately for most blokes all they came home to was the same staid world they had left. As Leonard Rossiter's character Rigsby said in *Rising Damp*: 'Permissive society? There's no such thing. I should know; I've looked for it.'

But the puritan stranglehold which had stifled life until now was changing slowly. Hugh Hefner was expanding his *Playboy* world; at the movies, Raquel Welch and Brigitte Bardot evoked a sense of real burning sexuality; and a sex scandal even brought down the British government. The genie was out of the lamp – and there was a waiting list of men eager for a good rub.

The movie *Alfie* came out in 1966. Michael Caine would, of course, always be a solid geezer in the pantheon of great retrosexuals and in the lead role he typified the attitude of his generation: 'I don't want no bird's respect,' the chancer exclaimed. 'I wouldn't know what to do with it.' Then, later on in the movie, he comes out with the classic line: 'My understanding of women only goes as far as the pleasure. When it comes to the pain I'm like any other bloke – I don't want to know.'

Pre-retrosexual Heroes

Lord Nelson
They don't make heroes like Horatio any more. He left school at 12 (I know – and was home in time for lunch) to join the Navy, eventually losing an arm and an eye fighting the French. As a commander, he gained a reputation for defying his superiors; fighting the Spanish, he ignored orders to cease action by putting his telescope to his blind eye and claiming he couldn't see the signal. And don't forget, he managed to keep the beauty Lady Hamilton on the go for six years while still having his Fanny at home.

Henry Wilmot, Second Earl of Rochester
Thought to have learned debauchery at Oxford University, where he went at 12, he became renowned at Charles II's court for drunkenness and putting it about. He fled the court after abusing the King in a poem and set up as 'Dr Bendy', a quack doctor dealing in fertility. He died of syphilis at the 33, but not before cunningly denouncing his atheism to a priest at his bedside.

Errol Flynn
The man who shares his coffin with six bottles of whisky lived his life as a total roister-doister. Expelled from school for fighting and, allegedly, having sex with the daughter of the school laundress, he went to Hollywood and continued in the same vein – giving birth to the term 'In like Flynn'.

Tasker Watkins
The Welsh would have their fair share of good blokes – Burton and Tom Jones included – but none can match the heroics of this Victorian Cross-winner. On an August day in 1944 he led a bayonet charge with his 30 remaining men against 50 Nazi infantry, practically wiping them out. Then, at dusk, separated from the rest of the battalion, he ordered his men to scatter and, after he had personally charged and silenced an enemy machine-gun post, brought them back to safety.

Len Shackleton
Without the Clown Prince there would have been no Bowles, Worthington or Gascoigne. Loyal to Sunderland (he said, 'I'm not biased against Newcastle; I don't care who beats them!' when that kind of thing was truly witty), he was a rebel; a chapter of his autobiography entitled 'The Average Director's Knowledge of Football' consisted of a single, blank page. A masterly ball player, of course, he was largely overlooked by the England team (the FA explained: 'Because we play at Wembley Stadium, not the London Palladium!')

Arthur Seaton (played by Albert Finney in the film *Saturday Night and Sunday Morning*)
Seaton was a right bastard, but he was a sign of British Man breaking free. A factory worker in Nottingham, he grafts six days a week and lets rip on the seventh in beer-drinking competitions and fighting. In a famous speech he explains: 'Mam called me barmy when I told her I fell off a gasometer for a bet. But I'm not barmy; I'm a fighting pit prop that wants a pint of beer – that's me. But if any knowing bastard says that's me, I'll tell them I'm a dynamite dealer waiting to blow the factory to kingdom come. Whatever people say I am, that's what I'm not, because they don't know a bloody thing about me!'

The 1970s – A Golden Era

And so we reach the sensational 1970s: a decade of industrial action, bloody and bitter conflict in Northern Ireland, the suffocating oil crisis, football hooliganism and a proliferation of brown slacks, jumpers and cars.

Top of the Pops was full of fey 'glam' boys wearing make-up (only punctuated by the 'risqué' Pan's People); you had to get up and walk all the way to the TV in order to change the channel to one of the two alternatives (all BBC2 had was endless Open University programmes on correlation coefficients) and wait an age for the telephone dial to rotate back to the top.

When you got out of the house, the pubs closed at 10.30pm, the mingling (and minging!) smell of overcooked vegetables, Embassy and Brut permeated everything and the rise of the disco even encouraged some blokes to make complete fools of themselves by attempting to dance.

Welcome to the Golden Age of Man

The 1970s man really thought he was 'it': a rough and ready, cocksure fella who'd no longer bow and scrape, looked up to no one and would give as good as he got. When we say 'retrosexual', this is the era we're harking back to: a time when blokes could stride out in the wide-lapelled suit and brogues, down a pint of Double Diamond and really believe they were cock of the walk.

Most working men – whether they were on the factory floor, on the buses or at the steelworks – would have been trade unionists. For the first time in history, they'd established decent pay, safe working conditions and the right to take a sickie every now and then when they fancied a long weekend. No manager going on about productivity and contracts was ever going to threaten them again: not when they had some aggressive Scottish general secretary no one could understand shouting the odds on the news every evening.

Their sex life was also a whole lot better and, with the television channels closing down at 10pm, it was just as well. At last women seemed to have got the idea of the permissive society and were willing to grasp the nettle (and more besides). The likes of Pan's People, *Last Tango In Paris* and Bet Lynch had all inspired them to be sexy, while the emerging feminism (mainly as expounded by Billie-Jean King every year at Wimbledon) and more responsibility at work had given them the confidence to take control of their bodies

It's tempting to believe that life was easier in the 1970s, when jobs were for life, when beer was 15p a pint, before HIV and compulsory condoms; and when shopping malls were something alien you saw on American TV programmes and never got dragged to, but it's men who've changed, not life. 1970s Man didn't fret over the nitty-gritty of life; he got on with it. Work, beer, football and sex were all that mattered to the single bloke and the rest was detail that would work itself out. It was a simpler life, because he still dealt with things like a man and women respected that. They might have wished he was a little more sensitive, didn't swear at her mother and didn't fart all the way through *Peyton Place*, but they admired the way he made decisions, took the knocks without whining and took control in the bedroom – and they've been missing it ever since...

1970s Man is our retrosexual template. Obviously times have moved on; our manufacturing industries have been decimated and every other man now works in IT, sexually-transmitted diseases have changed our outlook to safe sex – and, of course, no one really wants to wear a tank top any more.

That 1970s Look

Burton's Suit
Getting ready to go out was never easier. Everyone wore a Burton's suit, 100 per cent polyester with flapping flares and airplane-wing lapels, in a variety of colours – as long as it was beige or brown. Those with an ostentatious bent would consider a purple suit.

Kipper Tie
As garish as possible – preferably in unfathomable patterns of green, orange and brown – tied with as large a Windsor knot as possible (although James Bond said the Windsor was the mark of a cad) and the short end tucked into the gaping gap between the second and third shirt buttons.

Aftershave
Yes. Men wore perfume. But this was no feminized aroma; it was Brut, Hai Karate or Old Spice. They might have smelt like a rotting mattress on a tip, but men were persuaded by sophisticated adverts from Henry Cooper or Peter Wyngarde ('Smells great') that it would be better than the time-honoured sweat and Woodbine scent.

Jewellery
The 'Medallion Man' image was a bit of a stereotype. Men generally still believed chains and rings were for gypsies, poofs and Tom Jones, but the 1970s saw this kind of thing begin to take off in the form of sovereign rings ('Sovvies' – now a chav speciality!), and chunky wrist and neck chains.

Zapata Moustache
In the 1980s this large, bushy 'tache, which extended down the sides of the mouth, was as much a sign of being gay as a collection of Doris Day albums and – gasp – an earring. However, originating among radical students and folk singers in the US who were themselves imitating the great Mexican revolutionary, this statement facial hair was soon adopted by thousands of British blokes whose only use for revolution was to get pub opening times extended.

Hair
The barnet was worn long in the way that suggested the nation's barbers might have shut up shop for most of the decade. Grown to a length where it began to curl every which way around the collar, it tended to be thickest over the ears, giving the impression that headphones were being worn under the hair.

Chest Hair
Almost unbelievably, in these days when men actually shave their chests (and, no doubt, other parts), chest hair was once seen as almost compulsory. Where did they all get it from? If you didn't have a chest which resembled a welcome mat you'd better not bother opening that second button on the shirt.

Sideboards
Not the kind of furniture you bought from G-Plan, but what are more properly called sideburns were worn as long and as fuzzy as possible. The singer from Mungo Jerry had shown everyone how to do it on *Top of the Pops* in 1970 and it soon swept the nation. Of course, it depended on how good a growth you managed; Chelsea's Peter Osgood would soon be taking on all comers for Best Sideboards of 1972.

1970s Roll of Honour

The Sweeney's **Jack Regan** (played by John Thaw)
Shut it and listen. Regan was the quintessential 1970s man: a hard-drinking, hard-fighting, couldn't-give-a-shit guy from the days when coppers punched first and asked questions later.

Steve McQueen
By the 1970s, McQueen was the man: cool, quiet, but with a look in his eyes that told you not to mess.

Bobby Moore
How could one man be everything? A great footballer, a Jack-the-lad, a gentleman, a sex symbol.

Eric Morecambe
There were the clever-clever Pythons, the camp Frankie Howerds and the *double-entendres* of Sid James, but only one bloke could be funny without even trying.

John McEnroe
Tennis, eh? It was high time someone stuck it to them and his 'You're the pits of the world' rant did it better than anyone.

'Budgie' Bird (played by Adam Faith)
Just as we cried out for someone to lead us through the decade, along came this angst-free, ex-con Jack-the-lad, determined to avoid manual labour at all costs.

Brian Clough
The big-drinking football manager-cum-god was nicknamed Old Big 'Ead. If someone disagreed with him, he claimed: 'We talk about it for 20 minutes and then we decide I was right.'

Rod Stewart
The original lad-about-town, Rod and his Faces made the Gallaghers look like shandy-swilling Northern softies. Just a shame about the tartan.

John Noakes
What better role model could a young boy want than someone whose name rhymed with 'blokes', had no style or tact and was happiest leaping out of a plane or careering down the Cresta Run in a bobsleigh?

Johnny Rotten (aka John Lydon)
Could any other decade have produced such a sharp, snarling, ball of pent-up aggression as the spewing mouthpiece of the Sex Pistols? If nothing else, his punk movement spared a generation from having to dance to the Bee Gees at school discos.

A Kick Up the 1980s

Even in the late 1970s, there were signs that things were heading in a different direction. The election of Margaret Thatcher saw the nation embrace the kind of hectoring, asexual woman men had spent centuries hiding in the pub to avoid; Quentin Crisp's exhibitionist and defiantly gay *The Naked Civil Servant* was a hit on television and opened up a previously closed world; and the Equal Opportunities acts of the decade began to kick down the doors of the last male bastions.

The author would like to note at this point that he believes the improvements in gay and women's rights were welcome and, indeed, long overdue; he's not so keen on Thatcher, but that's another story. However, the problem for men up and down the country was that these signs represented a challenge – and it was one they basically cocked up big-time. Like a turkey shoving its own feet up its arse at the year's first airing of "Fairytale of New York", they never gave themselves a chance.

The 1980s saw closet doors opening across the country. Before then, people had realized gay men existed, but only in the theatre, in pockets of Soho or on *The Generation Game*. There wasn't really any discrimination; if one of that sort showed his face it'd be battered well before anyone had time to discriminate against him. And yet suddenly there was another kind of man on the streets, a gentler, more stylishly dressed kind (albeit often with a ridiculous, high-pitched, sing-song voice, but let's not split hairs). From being daring in their sexuality, they were now also daring and exciting in their appearance, and who could help but feel that straight men looked staid and boring in comparison?

By the end of the 1980s, every single woman would have their own GBF (Gay Best Friend) – someone who would not only fulfil some straight 'boyfriend' functions, but went shopping, was interested in clothes and even knew who shot JR. What's more, they never talked about football, didn't drink beer and never spent the evening trying to get in their knickers. Could it be that women didn't actually want – or need – a straight man around? After all, as they were constantly reminding us, all the best-looking blokes were gay.

So how were straight men supposed to react? The dating game had been turned on its head. Women suddenly seemed to be calling all the shots and many blokes felt the rug being pulled from under their feet. They were suddenly surrounded by worlds they couldn't understand, such as Greenham Common, New Romantics (Christ on a bike! Men wearing espadrilles!) and skin creams for men.

Then, in 1987, a low-profile event took place in North London that was to have great symbolic significance. The flagship branch of Swedish home furnishing store IKEA opened. Men had long been used to being dragged along to the supermarket on Saturday mornings and had developed many strategies for dealing with it, but here was something new: a whole great store full of just furniture. Lured in by the promise of a plate of Swedish meatballs, they soon found themselves lost in the kitchen section, clamouring for air in the bargain basement and looking at their watch every two minutes in the four-hour queue for the till. Visits to the store would break even the steadiest of relationships; couples would start arguing in the car park and be filling in divorce papers by time they reached bathroom fittings. For many men, it was the last straw.

As we headed into the 1990s, all the talk was of a new man for a new century: no mention of the fact that the last century's man had got us through economic depressions, world wars and regular World Cup humiliations. This 'New Man' would be happy to reveal his emotions, never raise his voice, be interested in interior decoration and soap operas, yet still manage to maintain an erection when requested: a kind of cross between Jeremy Paxman, David Cassidy and Jesus. Was that too much to ask?

In 1997, the death of the Princess of Wales marked another watershed in the history of British men. The solemn and dignified funeral was accompanied by something altogether more sinister: the deafening sound of grown men sobbing in the street. A sea change had swept through the majority of the nation's men; the Millennium was coming and with it a world of health and safety rules, ASBOs and caring, sharing eunuchs.

How, In The Name Of Humanity, Did We Allow This To Happen?

- David Bowie: Man or woman? Human or alien? Terrible actor or... well, terrible actor?
- *Brideshead Revisited*: Floppy hair and teddy bears? Spare us, please!
- Designer labels: Versace, Hugo Boss, those ridiculous crocodiles... What on earth was it about?
- Adam Ant: 'Ridicule is nothing to be scared of.' Lucky, that.
- Elton John: No one was shocked about Reg Dwight's flares, garish glasses or horrific pianos, but how we could have done without the moaning, attention-seeking and tantrums.
- Sir Ian McKellen: OK, you're gay. We heard the first time – now shut up.
- Celebrity deaths: Lennon and Elvis paved the way for the great Princess Diana cryathon as men somehow forgot how to 'get over it'.
- Jon Bon Jovi: Rock was about dirty denim, greasy hair and being an outlaw – not blow-drying your hair for three hours.

What Kind Of Man Are You?

Have you succumbed to the myth of the metrosexual? Are you more new man than old bloke? And do you need a testosterone injection before we carry on? Take this test and see just how far you have to go...

1. You trip over on the pavement causing a bad sprain on your ankle. Do you...
    A. Go to casualty and spend four hours moaning about how long you have to wait?
    B. Lie in bed with a cold compress for days and compose letters to the council?
    C. Call your lawyer and find out who you can sue?
    D. Call in sick for a few days and find a stick to limp to the pub with?

2. What do you find yourself spending the most time thinking about?
    A. The desperate and inevitable loneliness of the human condition.
    B. Who would win a fight between a lion and a grizzly bear?
    C. Lunch.
    D. An assortment of women in varying degrees of undress.

3. A hot date coincides with an important football match. Do you...
    A. Carry on with the date; it would be impolite to let the lady down?
    B. Call her and discuss the issue, giving her the ultimate decision?
    C. Go to the football; you can always see her another day, but it could be the game of the season?
    D. Go to the football, then the pub and call in on her after midnight on the way home?

4. You are clothes shopping. Do you head for...
    A. Armani: If I close my eyes slightly I can really imagine that I'm a rapper?
    B. Hugo Boss: casual gear but with a label that really impresses?
    C. Marks & Spencer: they do the whole lot and you can get a wardrobe-full in 20 minutes?
    D. George at Asda: six white T-shirts for a tenner in the trolley – job done.

5. You are heading out to meet your bird. You've just had a shave. Now it's time for...
    A. A moisturizer – it really brings out the softness in your skin.
    B. A dab of aftershave – just subtle enough to arouse her interest.
    C. A quick check that I haven't left any shaving foam behind my ear.
    D. A dump – there's nothing worse than getting a bird in bed and having to get up to evacuate your bowels.

6. Your girlfriend has asked you to prepare supper for once. Do you...

A. Present your signature dish – a lightly grilled, Thai-infused sea bass with lemon sautéed potatoes and a basil and rocket salad?

B. Throw together a delicious plate of beans on toast – with a cheese slice on top for a touch of class?

C. Rummage through the drawers for a Chinese takeaway menu?

D. Get a new girlfriend?

7. A new girlfriend leaves the choice of venue for your first night out to you. Do you...

A. Book good seats at the opera and a corner table in an intimate restaurant?

B. Throw your flatmate out, dim the lights, open a bottle of wine and put a Barry White CD on?

C. Take her to a pole-dancing club just to get her in the mood?

D. Ring your mates and find out what pub they're going to?

8. She takes you into the local coffee shop. Do you...

A. Order a tall skinny mochachino?

B. Order a herbal tea (you don't do caffeine after 7.30 in the morning)?

C. Whine, 'Can't I just get a normal coffee?'?

D. Demand PG Tips – and not bleeding English Breakfast Tea. In a mug. Three sugars?

9. Football – what's wrong with the modern game is that....

A. The inexorable compulsion to win has taken the thrills and showmanship out of the game.

B. It's been hijacked by the corporate prawn sandwich brigade. Some of them don't even sit facing the pitch, you know?

C. They outlawed the two-footed challenge.

D. You can't get a pint within five minutes' walk from the ground.

10. It's time for Christmas shopping. You prefer...

A. To very smugly do all your shopping online, in September.

B. Get everyone vouchers.

C. To go out late on Christmas Eve – you only have a few to get and once the crowds are gone it's really easy.

D. To have red-hot pokers shoved where the sun don't shine.

Answers:

- **Mostly As:** You love these questionnaire things, don't you, you pussy? I bet you spend most of your spare time reading your female friends' *Marie Claire* and working out whether you're an Autumn Person or a Spring into Summer. You make me sick. Why are you reading this book anyway? Sorry. Got a little carried away there.

- **Mostly Bs:** You like to think you're a little bit of a lad, just enough to tease the girls, but you're not above tagging along to their book club, 'working out at the gym' for half an hour every night and buying your Bento box for lunch. Come to think of it, what exactly are you: some kind of bastard love child of Graham Norton and Liam Gallagher?

- **Mostly Cs:** Well done. You've retained some of the male identity you were born with, but are you sure you're not worrying a little too much about your feminine side? Don't worry; lesser men than you have shed a few tears while watching *Animal Hospital*. Stick with us and you'll be OK.

- **Mostly Ds:** Yeah, great. You've sussed out this whole retrosexual idea. You're hard as nails and a real bloke's bloke. So what are you doing reading a book? Carry on reading, fake boy, and you'll find out.

Top 10 Metrosexuals/Übersexuals/Just Gay Enoughs

1. David Beckham: One man and his sarong. The original metrosexual and still the worst. Who hasn't tired of his 'I'm an inspiration to gay men all over the world' schtick (although, of course, they can look but they'll never get to touch)?

2. Jamie Oliver: He's a geezer and he's from Essex, yet he still cares deeply about the kiddies and can drizzle extra virgin olive oil like no one else around. Delish? Bollocks.

3. David Walliams: He's the hetero one from *Little Britain*. You might think he's gay, what with all that mincing about and dressing up, but you can be camp and straight, you know; you just look a knobend.

4. Lewis Hamilton: Looks like he's too young to have a licence, but that smooth skin, smart suit and ads for 'products' see him looking for a number one place in the list.

5. Gavin Henson: 'It takes two hours to get ready – hot bath, shave my legs and face, moisturize, put fake tan on and do my hair,' the Welsh rugby star told Jonathan Ross. 'I need my fellow-players to say I'm looking good; I need it for my confidence.'

6. Jude Law: It says here that Jude has a 'doe-eyed sexual magnetism' – ooooh! Watch out, Bambi. And does anyone else wonder what an anti-ageing oxygen facial actually is?

7. Kanye West: Because, naturally, in the ghetto, the hardmen are all purse-toting mincers with their own clothing range.

8. David Cameron: He wants to cuddle hoodies, save the earth and he rides a bike – until he's elected, peels off his face and reveals he's actually Maggie T returned to exact her revenge...

9. Chris Martin: We could just about put up with the dull music if only he didn't write 'Make Trade Fair' on his wrists in felt pen like he was still in Year Seven.

10. Peter Andre: Where to start? His oiled six-pack? His big pink wedding? His heartfelt honesty (he had a 'breakthrough', not a 'breakdown')?

2. TELL US WHAT YOU REALLY, REALLY WANT

WOMEN: WHAT DO THEY WANT IN A MAN?

Yes, this is the 21st century and women do have a new role in society, limitless ambitions and opportunities, and more comfortable underwear, but they're still as tied to their genetic roots as men. Just as they're unable to have a telephone conversation that lasts less than 25 minutes, are instinctively drawn to gossip about minor celebrities and are physically incapable of walking past shoe shops, so they're naturally drawn to the undiluted male.

Unfortunately, they too have been subject to nigh-on half a century of creeping unisexuality. Magazine articles across the years – from *How He Can Look Cool In A Kaftan* to *My Guy's King Of Our Kitchen,* from *Can Your Fella Cry Real Tears?* to *He Shares My Mascara* and from *How to Get the Best From Your Orgasm* to *My Mr Whippy Spreads It On Thick* – have managed to give them the idea that their ideal man minces around in a sarong, creating a delicious lunch from a carrot and two lettuce leaves, and spends the best part of the evening gently caressing a specific part of their body that even top surgeons have failed to detect.

And yet you can be sure that the first time the unisexual man walks into the room wearing *their* kimono or starts filling the wardrobe up with more than two pairs of shoes, somewhere – however deep-seated – they will feel an inner despair (recognized by scientists as a residual instinct inherited from the prehistoric female who suddenly realizes she's with the berk who has only twigged the 'gatherer' part of the whole hunter-gatherer idea and it's going to be berry delight for tea again).

Somewhere along the line, women have become confused about what kind of man they really want. A massive cranial malfunction at some point allowed them to view men as 'friends': people interested in their emotional wellbeing, hobbies, views on interior design and how much saturated fat is in a packet of crisps. Once this misconception was established, it became an obvious route for men to exploit for sexual purposes: a dangerous turn of events. Somehow the early days of, 'I agree, sweetheart, Mrs Attlee did look better in the A-line. Now turn over so I can take you roughly from behind' has led to the sad state of affairs of today's, 'Not now, darling, I've managed to download the Habitat catalogue. Come and look at this wonderful set of ramekins.'

For the retrosexual, this presents a difficult situation. You are – obviously – the type of man of most women's dreams and yet they've been forced to pretend to be repulsed by your ilk. Tricky, but don't despair. With a little subtlety (I know, it's OK, just a little) you can walk the tightrope of giving them what they think they want and being the man you know they desire.

What Women Think They Want

- For you to wear an expensive, poncey scent.
- For you to take a weekly trip to a hairdresser.
- To have twice-nightly discussions on where the relationship's going.
- To be bought random unexpected presents.
- To be taken out at least once a week.

What Women Want

- For you to give off a subtle whiff of testosterone.*
- For you to look like you've run a comb through your hair some time in the last month.
- Their choice of TV between 7pm and 9pm.
- Flowers, within a week of any birthday or anniversary.
- The bins taken out once a week.

What Women Can Do Without

- You taking up valuable bathroom time.
- Comparisons of their family with genocidal dictators or serial killers.
- To have to smell your farts in the bed before sex.
- You fumbling around beneath the bedsheets for an eternity when you can roll over and be asleep in five minutes and leave them to get on with the latest *OK* magazine.
- Your views on anything.

*This is unrelated to the smell of a sweaty ball-bag.

TODAY'S WOMEN: SOME GENERALIZATIONS

What do you really want from a woman? A lovely smile? A puppy dog who'll follow your every action with blind admiration? A right looker who'll drop her knickers whenever you've got a spare minute? You'll be lucky. This is the 21st century and things have moved on a little. Women these days come in a variety of categories that would have baffled even our 1970s Man. Equal opportunities, feminism, parenthood, plastic surgery and even the Girl Power bollocks spouted by the Spice Girls have turned the quiet little girls of yesteryear into confident, self-reliant, über-women who'll happily grind your bollocks to sand.

So while most men have been retreating into mousey figures frightened to express their opinions, women have become more rounded individuals loaded with self-respect. These days, if you're a guy looking at developing a retrosexual style in order to pull, you'll need to be a little cleverer: to understand where they're coming from and how they'll respond to your – ahem – charms. For this reason – and to try to give the book some intellectual depth – we'll take a look at the feminine types of the 21st century.

Good-time Gals

We're not talking girls as in school uniforms and pigtails, but real women-girls. Provincial students, secretaries and apprentice beauticians – you'll find them in the tackiest clubs in town, in the chip shops and trekking round Top Shop and River Island all of Saturday afternoon. These are sassy, spirited good-time gals who are looking for a quick shag in the pub car park rather than marriage. Sounds good to you? You bet. These, in some way, are your ideal retrosexual women. They're not after much more in a bloke than a good laugh, casual sex and free alcopops all night, and that's your (rather long) middle name.

However, your problem here is going to be image. These tend to be young, mass-fashion victim sorts and they're on the look-out for a well-dressed, well-toned herbert with a T-shirt advertising an American bowling alley that went out of business in 1962 and a six-pack that can only be earned by spending hours in the gym (not spent staring at the girls stretching on the mats). As your idea of exercise is likely to be limited to lifting pints and your sense of fashion is strictly off-the-peg, you're going to have your work cut out.

Little Miss Sunshines

Just an old-fashioned girl who's looking for a bloke just like the one who married mum (then ran off with the next-door neighbour when she got pregnant again), these should be meat and drink for the retrosexual. Not interested in a career (all they're doing is waiting for Mr Right), they're happy enough working in supermarkets and as PAs until they can get down to the serious business of sewing name tags on Junior's school uniform and chatting at the school gates. Their best friend is their mum and they seem to have enough grandparents to fill a shopper-hopper bus – and they all need visiting at least four times a day.

Now, you're just the kind of bloke they had in mind: a right bastard they think they can mould into perfect husband material. Like an irritating wasp, though, they're relatively easy to attract, much more difficult to shake off. The more you try to get rid of them, the lovelier they think you are. Ironically, developing a caring, metrosexual side might be the only real exit strategy. They'll have their mother telling them that you must be gay in no time.

It's Mzzz, Actually

Here's a challenge. She's a woman who knows her own mind, whose mindset has been shaped by feminism and the modern era. You might find her beautiful and attractive, but all you're going to get is confrontation and aggression. But here's the rub. She doesn't hate men. She actually finds them fascinating – the power, the arrogance, the brute strength, even the stray hairs venturing out of the nostril – but she's not about to tell you that, you sexist wanker.

She'll let you know that your mind's warped by centuries of male hegemony and Theakston's Old Peculiar; that you haven't got a chance with her unless you've got a degree in sociology and are willing to stand outside the library on a Saturday afternoon collecting for some nefarious animal liberation group. But her eyes are saying something different here. If you can communicate your 'I'm a man, I do what I do' persona well enough, you could be on to a winner.

Miss 'Darling' To You

Back in the 1970s work was a man's world made bearable by the girls in the typing pool and the motherly figure with the tea-urn, but times, unfortunately for us, have changed beyond belief. Often these days your boss is a woman, the majority of your colleagues are women and you even have to go and get your own tea. Now, you might be mistaken into thinking these are just women with the same challenges as ever – and the workplace *is* a classic pulling arena – but beware: every now and then you'll meet 'the career girl'.

Like something from *Invasion of the Bodysnatchers,* they look quite normal and you might even fancy them if you go for that Donna Karan suit look, but these are seemingly alien beings unlike anything you might have met before.

A retrosexual tackles one at his peril. She will be single-mindedly focused on work, willing to stab you in the back and will veer from being the most charming, easy-going girl to a cold-blooded, genocidal dictator in seconds. And if she invites you to do a 360-degree appraisal, it's not what you think...

He's In Bed By 8.30pm – Promise

Single mothers: they're a blight on our society. A generation of boys is being deprived of a father figure, young women are being forced into a hectic and overstressed life and children are missing a balanced and complete family life. All true, of course, but what a great opportunity to the retrosexual on the sniff. If you're looking for a quick one on the sofa, a fiery affair or – God knows why – a 'Here's one I made earlier' family, then look no further than the school gates.

Why would you be in with a chance? Well, firstly, they don't get out much. They're that desperate, they'll put up with virtually any bloke who won't scare the children. Secondly, you're undemanding. Accepting you're second place in her affections – so far below Junior in the league table that you feel you're in a constant relegation struggle – without whining like a love-struck coyote (or metrosexual) will earn you so much goodwill. And thirdly, and most importantly, your retrosexual qualities will, for once, be welcomed. What else would a young mother obsessed with the wellbeing of her emotionally-spoiled brat be looking for other than a steady and reliable old-fashioned bloke? Unless, of course, it was one of those that got her in this fix in the first place.

Is It An Organic Condom?

Over the years, women have had numerous and diverse obsessions – from getting their whites bluey-white to the annual 'Timfest' at Wimbledon – but the latest obsession flies in the face of the retrosexual and presents real problems for any dating opportunities. This is the eco-obsessive, the girl who, out of love for the world, the future of mankind and because it said so in *OK!*, will demand, and pay dearly for, an environmentally friendly alternative to everything and anything.

Now, let's face it, any retrosexual worth his salt wouldn't mind if the earth imploded tomorrow as long as he gets a blow job tonight. But this is a woman who, mid-fellatio, will demand to know whether your love juice is organic, Fair Trade and recyclable. Will your retrosexual values ever be compatible with this kind of lifestyle? Or might it just be that in her apocalyptic nightmare of world meltdown, she'll be grateful for the one bloke who refuses to get his knickers in a twist over the ingredients of a packet of crisps?

10 Reasons Women Want a Retrosexual

1.   They Just Can't Help It
Through years of sexual suppression, political correctness and over-exposure to Phillip Schofield, they might try to deny it, but deep down – sometimes really deep down – they're going to love you for just being a man. It's that easy!

2.   Clear Mind Envy
Anxiety, phobia, weak nerves – these are the burden many women have to carry with them on a daily basis. Men, on the other hand, rarely have to bother their ugly bonces with much more than where the next pint's coming from. So just imagine, if you were racked with pain about which colour socks to put on, you'd admire someone who sailed through life even if disaster and tragedy followed his every step.

3.   Decision-Making Process
It would be unfair to suggest that women are unable to reach even the simplest decision. After all, to function in life they must constantly make crucial decisions, such as latte or cappuccino? But for most women, decisions are made only after full consultation with their three best friends: their mother, horoscope and whoever's standing next to them. What they really want is a random decision-making machine they can then blame for any ensuing problems: a man.

4.   Arms And The Man
A bloke has very few physical attributes to offer a woman. Sex, of course, and an ability to fart on demand will always be of interest to the fairer sex, but that old-fashioned pure brute strength can be a dead-cert winner, too. There's no point lifting heavy objects for the sake of it – you could do yourself a mischief – but simple things such as pushing a battery-dead car or opening a jar of pickle will always win you some admiring glances.

5.   Out Of Sight, Out Of Mind
It's best to get this out in the open now. Even if you're a cross between Brad Pitt, David Beckham and Albert Einstein, women aren't generally going to like you. What you're aiming for is a window of a couple of hours now and then when they're prepared to tolerate you. Real men have a distinct advantage here: they're often not around. Playing football, in the pub, in the shed, whatever; if you're not there, you won't be irritating them too much, and that's points in your favour.

6.   Vive la Difference!
Never discount the pure curiosity factor. In a world where men have been so

feminized, a retrosexual is something most modern women will never have experienced: a bloke who answers back! A guy who doesn't pretend or even try to understand women! A man doesn't care what any woman thinks of him! You're something exotic and a constant source of surprises.

7.   Bathroom Time

To you and I, time spent in the smallest room is not valuable. Sometimes it's relaxing to take a newspaper to read while you crap, but, generally, I think we'll agree, it's a quick shit, shave, shower – then out. For the average female, the room has a different function. By creating a heavy mist of condensation, an intoxicating whiff created by a vanilla-and-snodgrass candle and a trance induced by staring at yourself for hours, they can create a small, fairytale world of their own. They enjoy and deserve this indulgence, and sharing their dreamworld with an over-pampered fop is a far more frightening prospect than having their reverie woken by the odd cry of, 'Open up – I'm desperate for a dump.'

8. Talking Bollocks

Men's bodies generate more than 20 times more testosterone than women's and it can be – and often is – used as an excuse for many deficiencies of the gender. Modern metrosexuals have made testosterone a dirty word, associated with violent criminals, out-of-control teenagers, drug-cheating athletes and Wayne Rooney's vein-bulging mush. But it is man's secret ingredient. Without it he is a passive, unexcitable dullard (anyone thinking Gordon Brown at this point?), but with it he's walking, ranting human Semtex: unpredictable, sexy and exciting.

9.   Man About The House

Men have spent many years creating a myth around their worthiness in the home. There are certain things far too daunting for a mere woman to attempt, like changing a lightbulb or carving the turkey. So successful have they been that many 'partners' have fallen into the trap themselves, so even the smallest practical ability, such as handling a tube of superglue with aplomb, can make you look like you're good with your hands – and you know what that implies, don't you?

10.   Doesn't Show Feelings

Women are sensitive creatures whose emotional state is constantly teetering on top of a precipice the size of Niagara Falls. At any given moment, if they're not in floods of tears then it's odds-on that their mother, sister, best friend, hairdresser or someone they just met at Weight Watchers is. What they want is a bloke whose mood swings vary from 'All right' to 'Yeah, I'm fine'; where the first sign of him being a little down is a missing hosepipe and the towels tucked under the garage door.

FINDING A WOMAN

For the single retrosexual the search for women takes priority over everything – with the exception of England World Cup matches after the group stages – and there's no situation which should deter you from directly assessing your chances.

As a retrosexual, you'll discover that finding the right woman to ask out is easy. Not being too choosey is a start. Not trying to come across as a Hugh Grant bumbling fool who can't get his words out helps. And being prepared to take 'No' – or even 'Not if I was as desperate as a leprous virgin in a nunnery' – as an answer is a definite advantage.

In The Office

The changing world of women's employment opportunities means today's man has to think on his feet. It's no longer just a matter of winking at the secretary when you're waiting to go and get bollocked by the boss. Now you'll have women colleagues, girls you're in charge of and even women bosses. The true retrosexual will consider this a challenge. Unable to fall back on power or status, he will rely on wit, charm and that great old fallback, dumb insensitivity.

Working The Street

At the other extreme, for building site and road workers life can still be like living in a 1970s bubble. Most of these guys are the original retrosexuals: tough, straightforward and in a fantastic situation to show off their physicality. But, unfortunately, the world has moved on. Modern women somehow manage to ignore the calls from four yards under their feet of 'Cheer up, darlin', it might never 'appen!' from a bloke standing knee-deep in what could well be sewage.

Pubs, Clubs And Bars

Without the smoke-filled bars, pints of fizzy Watney's Red Barrel and a Hamlet cigar in each hand, you'd think the retrosexual would be lost. But once again, when Old Father Time takes with one hand, he gives with the other. 'My God! It's wall-to-wall skirt in here.' you can picture would-be ladies' man Tony Hancock uttering on seeing an All Bar One with three women sitting quietly in the corner. These are no longer bastions of miserable, hen-pecked men but establishments where women feel free to have a laugh and a few ridiculously-named cocktails. And, wherever there are women getting drunk, there are blokes who might otherwise be overlooked getting lucky. This is where you come in.

A Woman's World

Modern life presents so many opportunities to meet women and for you to display your retrosexual credentials. Perhaps most interesting are your trips to 'the woman's world'. A retrosexual should never look weak, but in realms such as the supermarket and the launderette, you have the opportunity to affect a nonchalant ignorance. A humble 'Do you fry or grill this?' or an inquiring 'Does this powder go in that hole?' can get you a perfect introduction. Remember what you're displaying, though; the contents of your trolley say so much about your lifestyle. Avoid the pretentious (is it rocket, roquette or fancy lettuce?), load up with plenty of potatoes and don't hide your one-person meals. Imagine you're wearing a huge badge saying 'I haven't the faintest idea about cookery'.

A Typical Single Retrosexual's Shopping Trolley:

- Box of 12 cans of lager
- Bottle of Jack Daniel's
- Two ready meal curries – extra-hot
- Two tins of Heinz beans
- Two Pot Noodles
- Large bag of potatoes
- One large steak
- Toilet rolls
- Large slab of economy cheddar cheese
- PG Tips tea bags
- Six eggs

DATING

Dating has become an ever more complex operation. Once it was just a matter of grabbing a woman by the hair and dragging her back to a cave. A few hundred years later we'd progressed to asking her father if you could walk the ornamental gardens together and even by the golden age in the 1970s there were only a few girls who would, as they said, 'put out' on the first date.

Retrosexuals are naturally straight-talking and straight-dealing guys, but if they're not going to fall at the first hurdle they're going to have to play things a little cleverly here. The 'New Man' of the 21st century has once again muddied the waters and left everyone a little confused about their true roles.

You must assume that the Mr Right she's looking for is strong, self-reliant, protective and assertive. Now, it's quite possible that you aren't all – or even any – of those things, but there's no need for her to realize that at this point. She might also *think* she's looking for someone who's cultured, capable of cooking up a soufflé and knows who the prime minister is. Your job here is to paper over the cracks long enough to allow your bristling masculinity to shine through. Good luck.

First Date Basics

Most of you, I understand, will be old enough to have heard the following hints before and will be using or ignoring them whatever. However, this is stuff that never changes, so it's worth reiterating.

Firstly, say something nice about her looks in a way that's genuine but shows a lack of understanding, such as, 'That's a nice badge, brooch-type thing you're wearing'. You've noticed, but have made it clear that fashion's not your thing. Think carefully about what you're saying, though, and make sure it's genuinely nice; 'You don't sweat much for a fat bird' is not a compliment.

Secondly, be prepared to listen or at least pretend to listen. She's bound to rattle on about all kinds of stuff you've got absolutely no interest in – friends you've never heard of, 'amusing' stories involving her mother, 'fascinating' gossip about her gay friend – but try to listen and smile and nod in the right places. If you do drift off and start thinking about tomorrow's racecard at Doncaster, then the general rule is to nod twice and smile at 90-second intervals.

Thirdly, be assertive and take every chance to show her you're confident. At a restaurant, be prepared to order for her (unless she's going to get shirty about having meat for every course) and try to find some element in your meal you can send back. Your dealings with the waiter will need to walk a fine line between politeness and aggression. Try not to argue or shout, and definitely avoid throwing him through the restaurant window. Similarly, at the movies, you might consider whispering to your date, 'It's a little slow; shall we give the rest a miss?' rather than pushing past everyone shouting, 'This film's shite, let's get a pint.' There are ways and *ways.*

Then there's always the chance that she isn't quite the babe you saw through your beer goggles at 3am on the previous Saturday. How you're going to progress the evening depends on what kind of gentleman you are, but grinding your teeth and staring at your watch every two minutes isn't going to make either of you feel better. The true retrosexual would stand up and apologize, admit he'd made a dreadful mistake, pay and leave. However, lily-livered apprentices such as yourself might prefer to check the size of the window in the gents', assess whether you can make a less dignified exit and hope you never run into her again.

Assuming the evening has gone well, you'll need to think about what you aim to achieve. Are you hoping for a quick shag up against the wall and to get home in time for *Match Of The Day*? Or could this be a regular opportunity worth cultivating? Remember, you're in charge. Depending on the kind of woman she is, you may need to be subtle about how you articulate this, but on a first date be sure not to show any emotions (lust is fine), and unless you want her to think you're a wimpish pushover never, ever, arrange a follow-up date there and then.

Second Date

So you got on like a house on fire, you were shit-hot in bed and her friend hasn't rung to say she's going to throw herself in front of a bus if you don't marry her next week. Are you prepared to see her again? A negative answer makes things much simpler. You're a single bloke and not a serial dater. It was fun and if you bump into her again, you wouldn't say no to a repeat performance.

A 'yes', however, makes the whole thing a bit more complicated. No matter how much you might package it, a second date constitutes a relationship. You may be thinking, 'That was great sex, she only lives round the corner and she didn't even mind my farting in the bedroom,' but the chances are that she's thinking, 'He's an Aries and that's compatible with my rising Gemini, maybe we could go to my parents next Sunday, and I'm sure if I ask him nicely he won't fart in the bedroom.'

If you're prepared to put up with this, that's fine. There's no need to feel ashamed. Even retrosexuals can find themselves thinking an experience was pleasant enough to consider a return. However, how you act now can have a devastating effect on your future.

- Leave it at least a week before ringing her. If she rings you before this, mumble something about being busy, but don't go into details.
- Arrive, unruffled and without apology, slightly late for the date. There's no point being so tardy as to upset her, but 15 or 20 minutes should be enough to demonstrate your unreliability and independence.
- Dress down a little. Make it clear that you may have made an effort to impress on the first date but that's as far as it goes.

GOING OUT

Either you really, really like the girl or you're too lazy to go out and try to find someone different. Congratulations! You've found a fun companion, a friend you can trust, sex on tap and someone to sew the crotch of your jeans back together. You have, haven't you? Just in case, here's a checklist of things that could go wrong.

- She's left a toothbrush at your flat.
- She's often too 'tired' or 'busy' for sex.
- She doesn't like your mates.
- She likes your mates.
- She wants to talk about 'where the relationship is going'.

Your role is to be in constant denial of the existence of any 'relationship'. Whatever this is taken to mean – and its definition can be very varied – it can only mean a restriction of your freedom as a retrosexual. You are two single people who happen to enjoy each other's company, preferably in the bedroom. You don't need to share hobbies or interests, you have no obligation to disclose your whereabouts or plans, and there's definitely no need for you to be seen out together (although you're expected to be cordial if your groups of friends accidently meet in a social setting).

Some Retrosexual Sure-Fire Chat-Up Lines

- 'You wanna get a-going, so you can start a-blowin'?'
- Beckon a girl over with your finger, then say: 'If I can make you come with one finger, imagine the fun you could have with the rest of me!'
- 'If you were a burger, you'd be McGorgeous.'
- 'I may not be the best-looking guy here, but I'm the only one talking to you.'
- Stand at the door at the end of the night and ask any unaccompanied women if they need a man for the night.
- 'What has 148 teeth and imprisons the Incredible Hulk? My zipper.'

Quality Time

Quite the most baffling of new ideas is that of 'quality time' – the allocation of an evening or even a weekend day to be spent by a couple. Quality time, however, isn't what you think. It doesn't involve football, sex or the boozer; it does, however, invariably involve staying at home and doing something that she enjoys (but is usually perfectly happy doing by herself). It can include lying together on the sofa watching a crap film starring someone who used to be in *Friends*, drinking minuscule quantities of sickly sweet white wine or – and worst of all – talking. The latter can be devastating. There are very few subjects a couple can talk about without it ending in shouting, tears or the destruction of a fragile, tasteless but cherished ornament.

Dating Don'ts and Dos

- Do wear a clean shirt. You might not be a preening peacock, but you're big enough to look after yourself. It just means not turning up with a small portion of yesterday's dinner down your front.
- Do arrive at the venue first. You need to make sure it's suitable, romantic and that your mates aren't hiding around the corner waiting to have a good laugh.
- Do choose your meeting venue carefully. You might feel most at home in the bookie's or the lap-dancing club, but find somewhere you'll both feel comfortable – like the pub or an Indian restaurant.
- Do consider a trip to the cinema for a first date, but set the boundaries straight away: no romantic comedies, foreign films or anything with Ben Affleck.
- Do make it clear you're ready for sex on the first date (perhaps affording her a glimpse of a condom as you open your wallet). You probably still won't get it, but it'll stop her thinking you really do just want to be friends.
- Do agree to go on blind dates or set-ups – but make sure your phone rings after 20 minutes and that you have a believable exit strategy.
- Do insist on paying the whole bill. Going Dutch might seem like a good idea at the time, but you're setting a dangerous precedent of a fair and equal relationship – and there'll be serious and harmful repercussions.
- Do pay the bill in cash. Pin numbers are for nerds and bankers. The retrosexual is cash only; like him, it's straightforward, honest and only slightly soiled.
- Do make sure she gets home safely. Firstly, it establishes you as a proper gent. Secondly, you're being seen as the strong, protective type. And thirdly, you might just get invited in to check her boiler.
- Do ensure she doesn't have your correct phone number. Lie through your teeth about your number, your address and your name, if possible. Even the sweetest of girls has the capacity to turn into a bunny-boiler after a small peck on the cheek and it saves having to spend three weeks hiding in a tent on Dartmoor.
- Don't discriminate. All women are fair game and the retrosexual is always on the lookout.
- Don't hesitate. If it takes you more than two seconds to decide whether you fancy her or not, then don't bother. Move on.

- Don't stalk, beg or visit art galleries to impress women.
- Don't be frightened of rejection. Any woman may have her reasons, however unfathomable, for resisting your charms. And try not to be too rude; you might want to ask her mate out next.
- Don't have text message or email conversations. If it takes more than two sentences then you're turning into a wet sap.
- Don't have girls as mates – especially ones you think you're cleverly cultivating for sex after several years of being best buddies. Never find yourself cast as an 'honorary' women and don't go out on girls' nights out (unless, of course, there's a distinct option of multi-girl action).
- Don't pretend to be gay in order to get close to a woman.
- Don't seek attention. Never dance, make an idiot of yourself, perform a speech or, for God's sake, seek pity in order to get a woman to notice you.
- Don't get into a conversation about star signs; there's only one thing in ascendancy and it's down your pants.
- Don't ever say, 'I love you.' The three magic words are, 'A pint, please.'

SEX

Allowing ourselves to view matters from a women's perspective for once, the sexual prowess of the retrosexual is key. After all, someone whose stated raison d'etre is his masculinity has little else to offer apart from putting up a few shelves, and even those might have looked straight on the spirit level but look pretty wonky to the human eye. He can't afford to be so slipshod when the passion levels are raised.

Even here, there are modes of behaviour which, if ignored, could leave you being treated like a 14-year-old on his first visit to a brothel (of course, you're entitled to like that kind of thing but I'd suggest, that being the case, this isn't the book for you). Although eager to please and even more eager to please himself, the retrosexual is warned not to try, or even succeed, in doing anything in this scenario that might compromise him as he goes about his everyday life.

Foreplay

Get her to send a text when she's ready. You'll be down the pub.

Technique

It has been said that the key to great sex is knowing when to be selfish and when to be selfless. That's all very well, but women are varied and complex in their sexual demands and it's hardly worth the effort of second-guessing quite where your tongue or finger's meant to be at any particular point in the act. If she asks you to do anything specific, it's only gentlemanly to consider it, allow for any injuries you may incur and then generally continue hammering on the way you were before you were interrupted. This isn't to say you need to be inconsiderate; she might be appreciative of the trick you learned from a former girlfriend or from the football tour in Hamburg, although maybe not grateful for the accompanying biographical details.

You don't have to be on top to be in charge. Whichever position you find yourself in, think of your old man as the conductor's baton and the whole session a symphony. Where he points is where the action is and his strokes control the tempo. Keep it going as long as it's producing a sweet sound and be prepared to change it when it goes ugly or quiet. Build to your crescendo, then relax; take a bow. Now just wait until she's ready to go and put the kettle on.

Oral Sex

We have so far emphasized the dignity of the retrosexual, his respect for his partner and his refusal to demean himself. Such self-respect is, of course, at the heart of the true man. There is one exception: fellatio. You can never force a woman to go south, but virtually anything else is fair game. Beg, bribe, make promises you can never keep, even offer to be civil to her mother: anything to get her to drain the vein. Yes, you'll be less of a man, but boy, is it worth it.

And if she asks you to go digging for clams? It's a personal choice, but if licking the lips in the heat of passion is only going to ruin the enjoyment of your next cod supper then pass on the fish course. The author's experience has led him to suspect that the pleasure derived is minimal and that it could well be the result of a lesbian conspiracy.

Duration

Much has been made of the sexual skill of endurance, and those who have persevered thus far through this manual would be forgiven for thinking that this should be uppermost in the retrosexual's armoury. However, these are busy times and a man – and his woman – often have a lot of things to get on with. There's football on the telly, sandwiches to eat and, the truth is, it isn't always that easy to keep it going. It may be all very well for Sting and his 14-hour tantric sex sessions, but no amount of mental pictures of Camilla Parker Bowles can stop you shooting your load once the starting judge has signalled the off. Or is that just me?

Matchoftheday Interruptus

This can be the biggest sexual problem affecting a retrosexual man, as their sexual activity and performance can be adversely affected by hearing the *Match Of The Day* theme tune. Often they attempt to finish the job messily and immediately, or even leave the room, issuing a dismissive, 'You can finish yourself off, can't you, love?'

Fetishism And Other Options

So you've spent a great deal of time being just the man you want to be. What do you want to ruin it all for now? We've all done it in the heat of passion: worn a mask, snorkel and wetsuit while smearing chocolate spread across her ample behind, or dived off the wardrobe in a First World War fighter pilot's outfit on to a girl dressed as a 18th-century prostitute from the 11th *arrondissement*. 'Where's the harm?' I hear you cry. The answer is none – providing the whole sorry incident stays behind bedroom doors. But these are women we're dealing with: sexy, imaginative, seductive... but with mouths like foghorns. The next time you're wandering past Starbucks, you won't be imagining those giggles and whispers of 'Hi, Flipper' or 'Chocks away, Ginger.'

There are certain exceptions where sex beyond the simple 'Wham, bam, thank you, ma'am' might be acceptable to the retrosexual. Sexual action outside might spice up the action a little and could help raise your esteem in the community. The park, the pub car park wall and the back seat of the car itself all offer suitable venues. Of course, few of today's cars are as accommodating as the old Escorts and Cortinas – unless it's a Volvo and you fancy shagging a yummy mummy while her four kids play with their PSPs – and these days you'll need to make sure you don't set off any of your gadgets. Afterall, you hardly need the sat nav saying, 'Keep straight on and turn left at the next junction' at the moment of climax or the airbag going off just as it's time for a little tonsil-tickling.

Orgasm

There has been much debate over whether an orgasm is necessary to fulfil a sexual encounter. The retrosexual's answer is a resounding 'Yes.' The game isn't over until you've spooged. If you don't manage to shoot your load by the time she's put her skirt on, there are only three possible consequences:

- She'll be fuming and you'll be left with a hefty dry cleaning bill as she refuses to leave the house with your cocknog all down her gladrags.

- You'll have to launch the hand shuttle in double-quick time.
- You'll spend the rest of the day feeling like someone's tied a knot in it and that you'll never get a boner again.
- As for the woman – well, it's up to her. Too much has been made of a man's responsibility in this area. It's not a competition, and even if it was, my money would be on the mister spilling his jizz juice before the search for the G-spot ('G' for God Knows Where) has got under way.

Post-coital

The moments after ejaculation are crucial for the integrity of the retrosexual. You're bound to be engulfed by a tidal wave of emotion; of physical exhaustion, joy, despair, a search for the deepest meaning of life and a need to pee. All these – except possibly the last – will pass pretty quickly and your job is just to get through the 30 or so seconds in which you're likely to say or do something you'll regret. These can include:

- Whispering in a touching tone, 'I'm sorry.'
- Crying.
- Declaring undying love in a cloying voice.
- Enquiring how your performance rated.

Instead, your task should be to assume a silent reverie – picturing a freshly cooked full English breakfast will often do the job – emerging, as you regain your cool, into a self-satisfied smile. At all costs, avoid any kind of post-coital post mortem. As far as you're concerned that was a perfect 10 performance even if it took you an hour to get it up and two minutes to shoot skeet. In any later inquests you can argue the toss, but at this moment you are at your most vulnerable.

The other post-coital danger area is 'the cuddle'. For many women, the warmth of the after-sex cuddle makes it worth going through the whole grunting, heaving procedure, but for men it's a truly pointless exercise; it's going to be at least half an hour before you're going to be armed for action. Pause for thought, though; being a retrosexual doesn't mean being a heartless, unsentimental bastard, and a little investment for the future may not go amiss.

THE C-WORD

What's the biggest difference between a retrosexual and an in-touch-with-his-feminine-side, heteropolitan new man? Their contrasting attitudes to facial treatments? A willingness to vote for someone to be evicted from *Big Brother*? Or perhaps being able to buy a pair of trousers without having to try them on in-store? Nope. The crucial difference between the two is their attitude to relationships and commitment – words that barely register in the retrosexual's vocabulary.

Rule One for the Retrosexual is never to acknowledge you're in a relationship. You might have been married for 15 years, have four kids, a whopping great mortgage and a joint credit card that has the debt of a small South American country – but you must still refuse to admit to yourself that you're not some free spirit who could drive away into the sunset any time you want (if she wasn't using the car to take the kids to football practice).

Most women are perfectly aware of this situation and will try all manner of sneaky tricks to trap you into admitting you are, in fact, in a relationship. Such underhand and pretty unfair methods include:

• Trying to discuss with you which contraceptive method 'we' should use.
• Finding you an important role at their mother's 70th birthday party.
• Insisting on putting your name on the children's birth certificates.
• Waking you in the night to deal with a strange noise in the house.

Rule Two states that any retrosexual should be prepared to set out his stall regarding relationships from the off. It would be unfair on any woman to imply that you might want to hang around for more than 15 minutes after sex, but spelling this out for her there and then can often seem unfeeling and hurtful and, more dangerously, could lead to the offer to ride the baloney pony being rescinded. After the event, however, there are many off-the-peg excuses ranging from 'I don't feel ready to commit' (you don't have to add that, as a man, you probably won't feel ready any time this century) to 'You really don't know what I can be like' (implying a possible Incredible Hulk-without the-personality-type transformation) with some more personal lines including 'I'm only on remand to attend my mother's funeral' or, as a last resort, 'I'm having doubts about my sexuality.'

HOW MUCH HAVE YOU LEARNED ABOUT WOMEN?

What do the following sentences really mean?

'My girlfriends and I are going for a crazy night out – fancy coming?' *We love to have a gay man to pretend we're with when we're being chatted up by a minger.*

'Football! It's all so tribal – all you blokes getting worked up and chanting aggressively.' *I don't understand what you're doing, but that testosterone really gets me going.*

'Sassy 20-something looking for a guy with GSOH for movies, crosswords and long walks to country pubs.' *Overweight 32-year-old desperate for any bloke who'll show up with her at her friend's weddings and doesn't pee in the wardrobe when he's pissed.*

'He's great in bed – so sensitive to my needs and open to new ideas.' *Christ! He's such a wimp. If it wasn't for me he'd just lie there and read his book.*

'Don't you find passion is just a cosmic doorway into our inner consciousness?' *I will sleep with you, but only if I can spend the rest of the evening talking complete bollocks that no one else can be bothered to listen to.*

'Don't you think if we have sex it would just ruin the great friendship we've built?' *Haven't you cottoned on yet? It's your best mate I'm trying to get in the sack.*

'I thought you might like to come and meet my parents for lunch on Sunday.' *You and I have been going out for three weeks and are now as good as married and if you so much as look at another girl my Dad will come after you with a machete.*

'He's a bone-idle piss-head who struggles to heave his arse off of the sofa unless the remote has dropped between the cushions.' *He's just a normal bloke but I can't help but love him when I see that gleam in his eye and the roll of fat on the back of his neck.*

'I do so love having these cuddly Friday nights in every one in a while.' *And if you do manage to break out of those handcuffs, I'll blow your kneecaps off with this shotgun. You are not going to the pub again!*

3. WHAT WERE YOU THINKING?

The retrosexual is a man of action, an impulsive, decisive doer who fires first and asks questions later. This is part of what gives him the devil-may-care aura that women find so darned attractive. Now, my guess – as you're reading this book, you nerdy twat – is that you wouldn't 'do' even if someone wired 10,000 volts through your John Thomas. We're therefore going to spend a little time considering how you reach the state of intuitive action.

The modern man has been led to believe that a decision cannot be made properly unless it's mulled over, looked at from all sides and left to sleep on. He needs to consider the consequences for himself and others, and assess the chances of success, the possible repercussions of failure and what his mummy's going to think of him. Whether he's choosing to ask a bird out, buy a new motor or tell the guv'nor to stuff his job where the sun don't shine, it seems he needs an eternity to make his mind up.

The Government is just as bad. Where, once upon a time, they'd introduce a policy because it seemed like a good thing to do, nowadays they seem to need all kinds of think-tanks and focus groups to decide for them. This is the Government, elected to govern; if we wanted 20 middle managers from Cheshire to decide whether to knight Jamie Oliver, we'd have voted for them or started a revolution around a slogan of, 'We're probably not too happy about that.'

When John Wayne was lying prostrate, having been shot in the leg, and looked up to see the evil rustler, kidnapper, Injun or whoever pointing a gun down at him, he didn't stop and ponder the situation or get a couple of mates together for a chinwag and a bit of advice. No, he would intuitively roll over, throw sand in the bad guy's eyes, draw his pistol and blast him to kingdom come. After all, this is the man who once summed the whole thing up by claiming: 'If everything isn't black and white, I say, "Why the hell not?"'

Not, of course, that we're advocating blasting everyone away – although that could solve a few problems. It's just that since the golden era of the 1970s, the whole decision-making process has become over-complicated for the average male.

DECISION MAKING: THE MODERN MAN

- Is action really required?
- Could I be sued in a civil court as a result?
- What will my wife/girlfriend say?
- Is it environmentally friendly?
- Might I get a slightly disapproving look from a passer-by?
- Would I reach a preferred solution by writing to the local paper?
- What would Jesus do?
- Should I check I'm not infringing the local by-laws?
- Will my action be of benefit to the community, especially its disadvantaged members?
- Shall I just have a moan about it in my blog?
- Will I be offending any minority groups?
- Might someone tell my mum?

DECISION MAKING: THE RETROSEXUAL

- Will anyone die?
- Do I care?

BRAIN CLUTTER

All this is clearly a result of what scientists refer to as 'too much thinking'. The modern mind of a man is brimful of unnecessary stuff which has cluttered up his ability to think straight. For years, the only things men had to worry about were getting paid and getting laid (and, in the bad years, not getting killed by Johnny Foreigner), but now they've managed to pile more and more responsibility on our shoulders. We're supposed to worry about getting enough fruit and vegetables, about catching a deadly bug when you've only popped into the hospital because you needed a dump, about mortgage rates going up and interest rates going down, about what training is necessary to fulfil our career aspirations with the company over the next year, about the fate of a tribe in a country you thought was made up by Robinson Crusoe, about your mobile phone frying your brain into mush and about how the hell you're going to afford the child support when it all gets too much... There's so much treacle to wade through, it's hardly surprising that there's no one out there capable of making a snap decision.

If you think of a man making a decision, you need to imagine the brain as a spinning wheel of information. He needs to stop the wheel at the relevant place as quickly as possible.

The following wheel illustrates the brain contents of a typical modern man's mind:

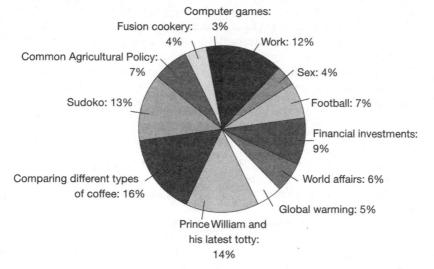

This compares unfavourably with a similar picture of a man's mind in 1974:

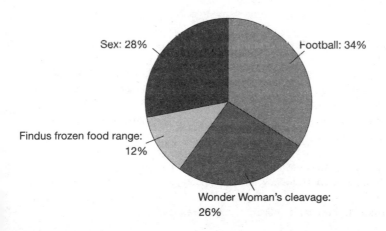

MATES, NOT MATES

As a retrosexual, you will not only be required to alter your relationship to women, but also to re-examine your behaviour and attitude towards other men. The modern man has adopted such a feminized outlook to friendship that a visitor from the past might believe we're all living in one big gay world. Walk around any town and it wouldn't be unusual to find straight men eating together at a restaurant, taking in a movie together and even sharing a trolley as they do the household shopping together at Sainsbury's. Behind the curtains, they're having 'lads' nights in', cutting each other's hair and attending book clubs. It might not be Sodom and Gomorrah, but it goes some way towards helping us understand how we've lost the respect of women across the nation.

You Ain't My Best Mate

The proliferation of male buddy films and TV shows might have given the impression that it's perfectly natural for men to have a male 'best friend'. But consider just for a moment the following: Butch Cassidy and the Sundance Kid, Starsky and Hutch, Batman and Robin, Ant and Dec – isn't there something a little strange about their relationships? And this was even before *Brokeback Mountain*.

In the real world, men over the age of seven just don't have best buddies. Sure, they have mates, perhaps some they see more than others, but no one you'd admit a weakness, spill your heart out or rashly lend money to. It's time to face the fact that as a Retrosexual you're truly alone in that big bad world: if the girls see you hanging with the same 'friend' for too long, they're just going to leap to the same conclusions you came to about Butch and Sundance.

How Not To Bond

Keeping yourself out of a close *mano a mano* relationship can, however, be difficult. Circumstances – such as work, sport, sharing prison cells – can throw men together and a basic human impulse seems to impel us to look for common ideas and aspirations over which to bond. To try to avoid this and adhere to the following guidelines:

- Try to keep times when you're alone together to a minimum.
- Avoid discovering another man's name for as long as possible and, when you do, don't use it.
- Never give your own name until absolutely necessary.

- Admit to no interests, hobbies, support of sports teams – and definitely avoid mentioning cars.
- If meeting in a sporting context, ensure you are never both naked at the same time.
- Do not give addresses or phone numbers and never make arrangements for further meetings. Keep things as vague as possible, ending conversations with a 'See you around'.

Let's Not Get Physical

Straight and gay men alike ought to be able to touch other men without sexual undertones or inference. They ought to, oughtn't they? Unfortunately, some people in our society are so myopic and strait-laced that they'll read anything into anything, so be careful. If you so much as brush someone's coat, there could be raised eyebrows. Besides, what do you want to go touching a bloke for anyway? Here are the few occasions when physical contact between two men may be overlooked.

- A firmly-gripped hand and two shakes are permitted on meeting and departing. Note: slaps, high-fives and touching fists do not count.
- One congratulatory hearty slap on the back is permitted after an announcement of an engagement, a birth, a divorce or a score of more than one hundred on the pub dartboard.
- Sporting congratulations can consist of either of the above or a simple, short ruffling of the hair.
- A playful exchange of punches to the arms and chest can often be innocent, but steer clear of wrestling, leg entanglement and any grappling which brings men's faces into close proximity.
- When officially accepted as being inebriated, a man can hug, lick and kiss any other man – provided he presents an apology within 12 hours of sobering up.

It Takes Two

All this is not to knock friendship at arm's length. It would be a solitary life if a man were to be completely friendless and there are many things two men can do together without having to feel a need to build a bond between them. These are:

- Fishing.
- Going to the pub (remembering to stand at the bar).
- Attending a sporting fixture – provided a visit to a pub or bar is included.

The following is a list of subjects you might freely touch upon in conversation:

- Football.
- DIY projects.
- Cars.
- Suggested routes between two random destinations.
- Accidents that have happened to mutual friends.

The following is a list of subjects worth avoiding even at the cost of an extended and embarrassing silence:

- Sex.
- Family.
- Work.
- Politics.
- Religion.
- Television shows.
- Other people.

Living With A Friend

Can a retrosexual share a flat or a house with another man? In an age where accommodation is scarce and pricey, it would be churlish to deny a man a roof over his head on the spurious basis that by adopting a certain lifestyle he's more likely to get his end away. This is, after all, the 21st century and people are hardly likely to judge your sexuality on your bachelor domestic set-up. How you and your 'friend' behave, however, could rule you out of the chick market, particularly if you appear to be too close or comfortable with each other. For this reason you should:

- Have separate bedrooms and ensure visitors are made all too aware of the fact, dragging them in to show them if necessary.
- Never cook or eat together. You should have clearly marked individual food cupboards and shelves in the refrigerator.
- Never be seen leaving the house at the same time.
- Never invite mutual friends round. If you act like a couple, you'll be seen as one.
- Never leave items of clothing in communal areas and never under any circumstances – not even popping round to the corner store for loo paper – borrow your flatmate's clothes.

THE RETROSEXUAL GUIDE TO PHILOSOPHY

Sooner or later, every man's thoughts turn to the basic tenets of philosophy. It may be at 4am when you're unable to sleep, when you're stuck on the hard shoulder of the M62 waiting for the AA to arrive or watching a particularly dull England away game being played in the far reaches of the former Soviet Union. Your mind will start to drift and the questions start to pop up: Who are we? Why are we here? Is there a God? Is there any point to life? Did I leave the iron on?

The instinctive reaction of a true retrosexual would, of course, be 'Who gives a toss?' But ignoring the fundamental basis of existence could cause problems in the future and possibly lead to drug addiction and alcoholism, inviting Jehovah's Witnesses in for a coffee or an unhealthy interest in golf. So here's a quick question-and-answer session to enable you to get on with just being a bloke – and, just maybe, help you impress the birds.

Who Am I?
- **Real Answer:** I am a member of a sophisticated, highly developed life form (insert your own joke here) with a unique ability to acquire intelligence, appreciate humour (even crap frat comedies) and be conscious of our own identity.
- **Retrosexual Answer:** I'm an on-fire geezer, an up-for-it ball of energy who'll take on anyone and anything. Unless it's before 11am, when I tend to yawn and drift off a bit.

Why Am I Here?
- **Real Answer:** I am either the random result of a series of coincidences that makes an episode of *EastEnders* look believable, the plaything of a higher power or heavenly body or a failed experiment dumped by an extra-terrestrial version of James Dyson.
- **Retrosexual Answer:** Because my mum got put up the duff by one of the men who came to fit the kitchen.

Is There a God?
- **Real Answer:** Is there any other explanation to the whole mystery of life than a divine, omniscient and omnipotent presence? Or are we fooling ourselves with a convenient and packaged explanation for the existence of our universe?
- **Retrosexual Answer:** I'm C of E. It says so on my birth certificate.

Is There Any Point To Life?
- **Real Answer:** We are here to live in harmony, make life more bearable for the rest of the human race and to heed the principles of the faith or political ideals to which we adhere.

- **Retrosexual Answer:** Nope. We're born, go to school, get a job, get drunk, get laid, get ill and die. Deal with it.

What Happens When We Die?
- **Real Answer:** Take your pick: we return to dust and never darken anyone's door again, we enter an afterlife dependent on our achievements and morality on earth or we return as anything from the president of the USA to a flea on the arse of a tramp.
- **Retrosexual Answer:** I'm going to come back and haunt the fuck out of anyone who owed me money.

A CRYING SHAME

Some scientists have claimed that until Victorian times it was physically impossible for a man to cry. Even if they had developed a rogue female impulse, the ducts were not sufficiently developed to enable tears to fall. This is not to say they didn't get a little choked up when their 19th child died in infancy or the Black Death wiped out the rest of the village or they stubbed their toe on a badly-positioned milestone, but generally they could disguise any grunts with a quick cough and get another round in.

Then came Charles Dickens with his stories of little orphan boys out pickpocketing, pregnant teenage girls giving away their babies and formerly wealthy good-hearted souls reduced to begging on London's streets. It was too much for one generation to bear and, whereas a hardier 21st-century mentality would have sent them packing with an ASBO, your top-hatted gentlemen of the time broke down and openly wept in the streets. It would lead to the Great Deluge of 1889 and the beginning of the modern drainage system (but that's another, and possibly a more interesting, book).

Somehow the gender – and this is an allegory, so it didn't actually happen – collectively managed to step outside, take a deep breath, light up a Woodbine and go back in pretending nothing had happened. It was just as well, as there were world wars around the corner which would test the mettle of even the most stony-hearted soul. Just imagine how quickly Adolf would have sent his stormtroopers over if our brave boys had blubbed every time Vera Lynn had started caterwauling over the airwaves.

The British man had regained his reputation. Across the world we became admired for our stiff upper lip and complete lack of emotion. 'There goes Signor Higginbottom,' they would chirrup in some Italian square as a gent strode purposefully by, tipping his hat to all he encountered. 'Who would know that his wife and children had died in a tragic car crash just half an hour ago?' Around the globe they were bemused by our lack of sporting passion ('There's Matthews, apologizing to the Belgian keeper as he tucks away England's fifth.') and the women of every nation soon grew to respect the coldness of an Englishman's touch and the way he would keep his socks and hat on in bed.

And so it continued, right on through the 1970s and 1980s. Even as England – and Scotland – crashed out of World Cups, much-loved members of the Royal Family shuffled off and Ken Barlow got repeatedly dumped there was nary a quivering lip nor a lump-in-the-throat clearing cough. British men were clearly made of sterner stuff than their continental counterparts and British women loved it; these were rocks against which the waves of their passion and hysterics could meaninglessly crash (that's nearly poetry, that is).

But, as we now know, as the turn of the Millennium grew nearer the wind changed. Men were harangued for their lack of passion, for failing to show enough interest in their partners' emotion and, for the ultimate crime, keeping a lid on their own feelings.

Bottling It Up

Yep, forget corporate manslaughter or perjuring yourself in court when, as a major author and politician, you've been caught red-handed – the major crime committed by men in the late 1980s was not revealing their emotions. It seemed that all of society's evils – bad parenting, domestic violence, post-Beatles Paul McCartney songs – could be put down to this basic lapse in human behaviour by half of the population.

How had the male population got it so wrong? Why, oh, why, when presented with the BEF's retreat from Dunkirk, did Winston Churchill respond with his 'fight them on the beaches' speech when he could have stamped his feet and screamed: 'I so hate that Hitler! It's just not fair. He's always picking on me'? And when Bobby Moore lifted the Jules Rimet Trophy with a dignified, wry smile, could he not have burst into tears, snogged the Queen and climbed through the Wembley stands in search of Tina and his adorably cute children?

For, suddenly, this is what men were expected to do – and some wet sops, of course, just couldn't wait. Gazza produced his fountains of self-pity juice after getting booked just before England crashed out of the 1990 World Cup finals, Stormin' General Norman Schwarzkopf broke down at a Christmas Eve ceremony in front of his troops, 'Iron' Mike Tyson bawled like a baby between getting a pummelling by Lennox Lewis and, to cap it all, Tony Blair wiped away a tear in his oh-so-natural announcement of Princess Diana's death.

The Kleenex® For Men Crying Game Report told us that 90 per cent of women and 77 per cent of men thought it had become more socially acceptable, over the past 20 years, for men to be seen crying. Apparently we cry to anyone from our partners, our female friends(!) and our mums to our bosses, female colleagues and the bloke who rings up selling insurance with a heavy Indian accent who says his name is Bob. So what are they getting so upset about? The following list goes some way to revealing just what can set off a bloke's waterworks.

- Death of a close friend or relative.
- A sad moment in a movie.
- Missing the last bus home.
- Accidentally walking into groin-height bollards.
- An argument with a girlfriend.
- Friends calling you names alluding to physical features (e.g. Huge Conk, Four Eyes, Tubby, Buster Gonads).
- Reminiscences of childhood trauma such as neglect, spanking or the day your dog trod on three of your Subbuteo players.

The situation is, however, very different after a night's drinking. In this situation many men have admitted shedding tears after:

- Spending three hours listing every past girlfriend and why they left.
- Spilling their pint, missing last orders and finding the chip shop closed.
- Their new best mate refusing to reciprocate in a full bear-hug.
- Remembering the dog (but not its name) that they swapped for a power tool.

THE RETROSEXUAL WAY

It's a hard life and every man has to find his own way of facing up to the knocks and setbacks of life. But the retrosexual will always remember that he is a man first and a quivering blob of jelly last. Women are no longer looking for a bloke who goes all gooey at the sight of a kitten, or comes home from work with a three-hour whine about how he was blanked at a meeting. The new woman wants a man who has some mystery; who, when you look in his eyes, won't reveal whether he's lost a leg or found a winning lottery ticket.

Here are a few very simple pointers to the emotional signs given off by the retrosexual.

- The retrosexual must never cry in public.
- The retrosexual may cry when he is sure he is alone in the following two instances: the death of a faithful dog or his team's defeat in a cup semi-final (so much worse than the final – you don't even get the day out).
- When asked how he's feeling, the retrosexual will always respond with 'All right', whether he is elated, in despair or has *beri-beri* fever.
- At the funeral of his mother, the retrosexual is permitted two throaty coughs – preferably taken during a hymn to provoke minimum attention.
- The retrosexual refrains from yelling, 'Jesus, Mary and Joseph!' or other exclamations at the point of sexual ecstasy.

Role Models

The true retrosexual will shun role models. He is his own man, does things his own way and doesn't need a pampered star to show him what to do. However, an apprentice retrosexual might appreciate a look at who out there is doing it and what they could do better.

Andrew Flintoff

The Lancashire and England cricketer became a summertime hero in the 2005 Ashes series, more than matching the Antipodeans' spirit and bluster, and then drinking with them in the dressing room. He followed this up by demanding beer off the Prime Minister and taking a pedalo out to sea at 4am. Given the freedom of his home town, Preston, he told reporters, 'That means I can drive a flock of sheep through the town centre, drink for free in no less than 64 pubs and get a lift home with the police when I become inebriated. What more could you want?' Exactly.

Jeremy Clarkson

TV's Mr Opinionated might be considered obnoxious, loud-mouthed and downright rude, and let's not forget his offensively tight jeans, but at least he says what he thinks and doesn't worry about who he is going to upset. Which is just as well, as it includes more or less everyone. A refreshing honesty or a God-given talent for winding people up, this is the man who said: 'We all know that small cars are good for us. But so is cod liver oil. And jogging. I want to drive around in a Terminator, not the heroine in an EM Forster novel.'

John Prescott

Call him 'Prezza', 'Two Jags', 'Two Shags', or 'that fat Old Labour git', but this is the man who single-handedly stopped Blair and Brown taking New Labour into a stratosphere of slimy metrosexuality. As a former cruise steward, he had to stand the patronizing jibes of 'Mine's a G&T' from the Tory benches, but Prescott was made of sterner stuff. This is a 21st-century politician who had a love for gas-guzzling luxury cars and belted a farmer who threw an egg at him (see colour plate section).

John Smeaton

Glasgow Airport's baggage supervisor was having a sneaky fag break when a burning Jeep Cherokee, which was doused in petrol and packed with gas cylinders, crashed through the window of the departure lounge. When confronted by the two Al Qaeda operatives, did he run, scream or call for help? Like f**k he did. He later said his first thought was: 'What's the score? I've got to get this sorted.' And then he laid into them, reportedly shouted, 'Fucking come on then!' and aiming a kick at the now deceased Kafeel Ahmed. Who needs Bruce Willis in a vest?

Russell Brand

The shaggy, backcombed, eyeliner-wearing, preening comedian might seem out of place on a list of blokey heroes, especially as he's a vegetarian yoga-lover as well, but anyone who's voted *GQ*'s Least Stylish Man of the Year (a year after winning the most stylish award) and wins the *Sun*'s Shagger of the Year award must have something going for them. You need more? Here's a man who shagged Kate Moss and doesn't boast about it, got sacked from MTV for dressing as Bin Laden on September 12, 2002, riled 'Saint' Bob Geldof and, rather wonderfully, describes himself as a roaring heterosexual.

10 Films That Made You Get The Tissues Out
(You Know What I Mean)

According to the Kleenex® Report, more men actually shed a tear over sad moments in a film than over the break-up of a romance or relationship. Are you guilty of misusing a tissue during a film? If so, I bet it was one of these...

1. **Field of Dreams:** 'If you build it, they will come.' Didn't work for the Millennium Dome though, did it? Then Costner's dead father emerges from the corn for a quick game of catch. And this means what, exactly?

2. **Bambi:** You're a grown man; you can stop sobbing. It's a cartoon, that's the law of nature for you and it's just a baby deer – and it's lovely with a little mushroom sauce.

3. **Ghost:** Are you blubbing because you hope she'll see some resemblance in you to Patrick Swayze or because you just can't bear to hear 'Unchained Melody' again?

4. **ET – The Extra-Terrestrial:** Face it; you don't even like your boy talking to the chav kids down the road, let alone an alien. But Elliot gets pally with a cute creature from another planet and it's all so touching.

5. **Gladiator:** You thought you were safe going to see a film about fighting and honour, but when Maximus bites it, I bet you blubbed like a baby, you big wuss.

6. **Saving Private Ryan:** Is war worth it? Man's inhumanity to man, the meaningless deaths, the futile comradeship and the sentimental codswallop like this that it inspires. It's war; people die. Get over it.

7. **Dead Poets' Society:** That's right. Do as the teacher says: 'Seize the day', live boldly. What? He's talking about writing poetry? This is a school where no one titters when someone says there's a character called 'Titania'.

8. **Titanic:** When Leonardo DiCaprio plunges to his death, most of us would have been secretly pleased that the smug git had got his comeuppance, but just in case there were any fellas with those heavy red eyes, surely a blast of Celine Dion cleared them away?

9. **Forrest Gump:** Don't tell me – you also blub at the bloke with wobbly legs coming in last at the marathon, school plays when your kid isn't even in them, and when they carry their baby around at the end of the Cup Final.

10. **Rocky:** You were there pounding the meat with him, weren't you? Taking every punch as he took on Apollo Creed? Then you had to ruin it by bursting into tears as the champ calls for Adrian.

Shaun Ryder

The pop world's full of rebels and characters, but can any match the full-on antics of the Happy Mondays' singer, the man who put the 'Mad' into Madchester and E into everything? Inspired by Johnny Rotten, and Liam Gallagher's inspiration himself, The Ryder took them all to the cleaners with his levels of debauchery and obnoxiousness. And if the man wants an epitaph, how about the line in Channel 4's compliance guide following his four-letter outbursts on *TFI Friday*: 'Please note that the Channel 4 Board has undertaken to the ITC that Shaun Ryder will not appear live on Channel 4.'

Ray Winstone

Actors – they're our role models, aren't they? But you look across the self-centred, puffed-up audience at the Oscar ceremonies or at the ranks of pretty soap boys and it's hard to find one with the gumption and honesty of a real man. So here's Britain's own Ray "I'm the Daddy now" Winstone. Not only are his roles in *Scum*, *Sexy Beast* and other movies true-to-life characters, but he's got a refreshing attitude to the ponciest of professions: 'What a ridiculous way to earn a living: dressing up pretending you're someone else. Get a proper job, son.'

Paul Scholes

Quite possibly the most under-rated player ever to play in an England shirt, Paul Scholes is as gifted as Gascoigne, Gerrard or Rooney. His performances with Manchester United have often overshadowed those of Giggs, Beckham or Christiano Ronaldo, but when was the last time you saw his ginger bonce on a 'personal grooming' advert? You never see him whine or moan, and he gave up playing for the national side when his efforts were not fully appreciated. Being a retrosexual isn't just about drinking and shagging; it's about conducting yourself as a solid bloke, and Paul Scholes does that in the media spotlight.

Bob Crow

In the 1970s, Britain had the finest trade union leaders in the world; scruffy, aggressive and with unintelligible regional accents, they were real blokes. Today's equivalents are generally smart-suited intellectuals hardly discernable from the Tory Eton brigade. But step forward Bob Crow, the railway workers' union leader, former card-carrying Communist and Millwall FC supporter whose straight talking ('I've got a simple philosophy on life; I say what I think and people either agree with me or they don't') has increased his union's membership and whose industrial action has, gloriously, pissed off the Home Counties' commuters.

GREAT RETROSEXUALS

THE SWEENEY: these guys defined the meaning of
Retrosexual for a decade. Better cultures than ours
would have made gods of George Carter (centre) and
Jack Regan (right). Note: lunchtime pub strippers were
so popular in the 1970s that many men would forget they
didn't even have a pint in their hand.

ABOVE: Now John Wayne knew how to treat a lady…

RIGHT: What a man? Alfie could pull even when paralytic (while you struggle to order a doner kebab).

ABOVE: Motor Mouth. If you're good looking enough you can get away with saying anything.

RIGHT: Is this how we want to see our sporting heroes? YES!

OPPOSITE TOP: "Due to industrial action there is no service from Tonbridge Wells." Can you see his heart bleeding?

OPPOSITE BOTTOM: Prezza: Now that's what we politicians call a "healthy debate".

NOT GREAT RETROSEXUALS

Raleigh brought us fags, chips – and gave the Spanish a kicking.

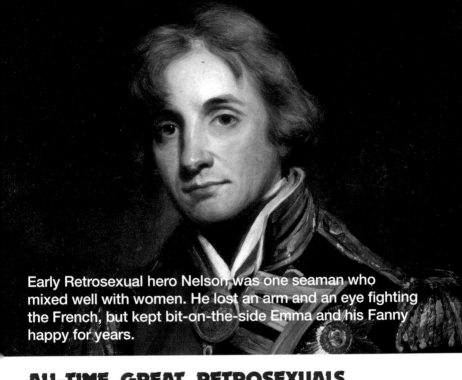

Early Retrosexual hero Nelson was one seaman who mixed well with women. He lost an arm and an eye fighting the French, but kept bit-on-the-side Emma and his Fanny happy for years.

ALL-TIME GREAT RETROSEXUALS

RETROSEXUAL WHEELS

LEFT: The retro look: nice.

RIGHT: Try to look as if you might have some idea what's wrong but for God's sake don't touch anything.

BELOW: The Sierra Cosworth 4x4 is the ultimate in classy wheels. It was (cos) worth waiting until the 1980s for one of these monsters.

RETROSEXUAL LIFESTYLE

Just carrying the heavy shopping bags isn't enough to impress some women.

A man who evidently has it all – no shirt required.

What do the girls find so attractive about this man?
A) His scarf?
B) The way he holds his hips?
C) The colour of his MG?

Getting ready to party, 1970s style with all that entails: strides that are skin-tight at the top with enough room to hide a couple of monkeys at the bottom.

This was what your local was like before they removed its soul and put in wall-to-wall mirrors.

They have all chosen correctly... now it's your turn –
where do you pee?

"Who could resist...?"

The perfect night out – watching the strippers with a fag and a pack of KP.

In the right light any woman can look beautiful.

Look at the life you could lead if you follow the
Retrosexual code.

Douglas Bull
is an unsung hero...

He's one of the unknown men
who perform dangerous
stunts in films, standing in for
the stars; and he's got the
scars to prove it. As a relaxation
from movie mayhem, he
buys his clothes from Hornes.
We've fitted his 46" chest
with this matching beach set.
The shirt costs £8.75 and
the shorts, £3.20. It's an easy
outfit for an active man...

Every man should know how to carve.

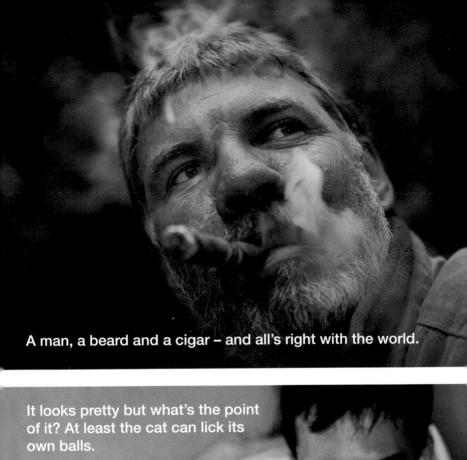

A man, a beard and a cigar – and all's right with the world.

It looks pretty but what's the point of it? At least the cat can lick its own balls.

Sporting wrongs (BELOW and RIGHT) and rights
(BOTTOM RIGHT).

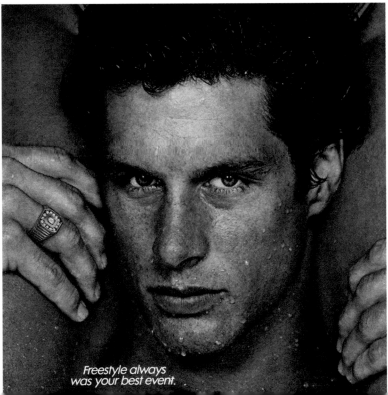

Freestyle always was your best event.

Physical contact between men is a complex issue – unless you're pissed.

"Yep, just as I thought." A real man is never lost.

Beer and men. What could possibly go wrong?

All dressed up and ready to go.

Robbie Williams
Robbie's a right bloke. He has no right to be, really; he's been in a boy band, pranced around on stage like a fool and dropped all kinds of hints that he might be gay, but he's never fooled anyone. Deep down he's just a football-loving beer monster, and don't we love him for it. Alleged to have shagged more female celbs than this book's lawyer would care to mention, and many more besides, he also cracked the fabulous line: 'I'm the only man who can say he's been in Take That and at least two members of the Spice Girls.'

THE NAME GAME

For working people, naming a boy child used to be so easy. He took the same name as his father or, if that was already taken, one of his uncles. Generally, you'd be called John (or Jack for short – how did that work?), Tom or William. We got on fine for years like that. When someone called out to the field, 'John, your ploughman's with farmhouse Stilton's ready,' you never got two hundred of them stampeding across the farmyard. They'd instinctively know if it was Jack's John, John's John or Tom's John who was being summoned.

But, like nearly everything, somewhere along the line it went wrong. Some bloke had to nip to the lavvy during a christening and when he got back he found out his wife had named the poor blighter Quentin. Naturally, the local womenfolk were excited by such a development and, thinking what a unique individual their son would be, had soon populated the world with Adrians, Justins, Julians and one Jeremy (although she was soon sent into exile).

By the late 20th century, the choice facing parents had grown ever wider (fortunately the fad of making names up – such as Drex and Vim – hadn't caught on yet) and some boys copped it pretty badly, being forced to grow up in constant denial of being gay, swotty, unpronounceable or – and this touched many a sore nerve – middle-class.

The height of new man-ism gave them a brief respite as effeminately-named men attempted to walk proud. Why, they asked was Tim any softer a name than Jim? Why could a Dave swagger but a Simon only cower? Just because his name was Kiefer, could he not share a pint with a Kevin? The answer came just as the new millennium broke: No. Fuck off back to the Home Counties, you mincing ponces.

The retrosexual is made of sterner stuff. No one tells us what to do; no one judges us but ourselves – and besides, it doesn't do any harm to change your name. Think about it carefully. You can only do it the once and it's best to do it legally. You don't want everyone to know you as Gary, only to come round your gaff one day and discover your post is all addressed to 'Meredith'. And tell your parents. Your new-found girlfriend could go off you if she picks up the phone only to hear someone asking if Roland's around.

You should instinctively feel what's right when selecting your retrosexual name, but in case you really are a right Nigel, here's a little guide.

- If you're not sure about whether to keep your own name, try yelling it across a crowded bar a few times. See how embarrassed you feel and what kind of looks you get.
- Don't try to shorten your existing name. Trist, Ade and Jez are fooling no one. Lose it and get as far away as possible.
- Your new name should only have one syllable, unless given a '–y' ending such as Gary or Billy.
- If you want to come across as a slightly dull but solid, dependable, salt-of-the-earth type, try John, Tom, Bill, Pete or Dave.
- If you fancy more of an 'I'm a bit of a laugh, me, if slightly unreliable', try Steve, Gary, Billy or Mark.
- Avoid Kevin, Dean, Trevor or Dmitri: fine retrosexual names, but you really need to be an expert to carry it off. Amateurs should beware that it could blow up in your face.
- Don't do nicknames. If you're a black rapper living in the Projects you can call yourself Droog, Decks or Jazz; if you're a white accountant living in Basingstoke you're just going to get people saying 'What?'

THE RETROSEXUAL CODE

Just as you were thinking, 'It's great, this retrosexual game. I can be as slobbish as I want, take no interest in anything even slightly feminine and still get laid on a Saturday night,' I'm about to ruin it. There's always a catch, and here it comes. One of the reasons women are prepared to sleep with men like you is because you remind them of their fathers: not the carpet-of-grey-hair-coming-out-of-his-ears part, nor the 'hang the asylum-seekers' ranting part of their father, nor even the father-who-ran-off-with-his-secretary-when-she-was-12-but-came-back-when-he-felt-guilty part, but the mythical man she always made out to herself he really was. You've just got to be him. It's easier than it sounds. Just learn the rules and stick to them (even if you feel like David Niven in some 1950s feelgood movie).

The Retrosexual Rules

- A retrosexual always pays for the date. If she tries to insist, so much the better. He still pays.
- A retrosexual opens doors for a lady, even if he doesn't fancy them. You never know who's watching.
- A retrosexual always carves the Sunday roast. Make sure you know what you're doing: practice on the cat, buy an electric carving knife, spend an hour taking notes at the kebab shop.
- A retrosexual always stands in the pub. Seats are for couples and people reading the *Guardian*, bar stools are for the pewter mug 'I'm mates with the landlord' drinkers.
- A retrosexual refuses to see the doctor even if he has a rare tropical disease that means his dick is about to drop off. He is, however, allowed to make sure everyone is made aware of how much he is suffering with a common cold.
- A retrosexual will remain silent when with his girlfriend's/wife's parents, staying in the room for at least 12 minutes before finding an excuse to leave.
- A retrosexual is never seen in the passenger seat of a car, unless it is a mini-cab, in which case he will ask the driver if he may sit in the front.
- A retrosexual deals with it. Flat car batteries, house break-in, cable TV malfunction, earthquake damage – don't put your head in your hands and cry; it's down to you.
- A retrosexual's friends will not come into the house. They may enter a shed or garage, but generally stand on the porch hopping from one leg to another.
- A retrosexual gets over it. Depression is an illness. It can be cured with a mixture of alcohol and aspirin. You don't need to pay good money for a shrink to tell you your father made you feel like a loser; you can remember that all too clearly in times of sobriety.
- A retrosexual should have at least one good wound, with an accompanying story which lasts at least five minutes.
- A retrosexual knows how to tie a Windsor knot when wearing a tie; he does not know how to tie any other knot.
- A retrosexual has a complete set of tools and at least three kinds of power tool, which he is often seen handling, if not actually using.
- A retrosexual will always give up his bus, train or tube seat for a pregnant woman. (To be safe, stand for all women; some look pregnant but will get upset if you ask when it's due.) He will then glare around at the other so-called men still in their seats with a look of sheer contempt.

4. LIVING THE RETROSEXUAL LIFE

HOME IS WHERE THE BED IS

The decor of the metrosexual's home is his statement to the world. His choice of colour, his theme, whether modernist, Oriental or black and chrome, his selection of wall art, all contribute to announcing what kind of man he is: a prick. In contrast, the retrosexual knows there are only four things you need in your 'crib': a fridge, a microwave, a sofa, a bed.

In the past, many skills were split along gender lines. Women knew how to sew, cook and give good blow-jobs while men could hit things hard with shovels, but the blending of identities has left women as bereft as men. These days, the only thing they truly believe they can do better than a man is home décor – challenge them and you're entering severely choppy waters.

For this reason the retrosexual deliberately avoids any attempts at making his flat or house homely, trendy or individual. Of course, no one wants to see a pig-sty, but short of putting up a big sign on the door saying 'Desperate horny bloke lives here', you can do no better than to create a completely male domain. But remember you're a bloke, not a student or a lad, so chuck out any 'borrowed' road signs and tear down your tacky football posters and old *Loaded* centrefolds.

Demonstrate your lack of taste

If you're lucky this won't be a problem. Any furniture you have will have been collected from skips or secondhand shops, or will be imaginatively used beer crates. Just ensure that nothing matches. Try to look at the colours in your home like a blind man might. Don't be scared to mix browns, blues and greens, and avoid pastels and bright colours. A visiting woman will always reach some theory about what you're 'trying to do', but deny any such idea vehemently.

Themes

Although seldom featured on *Grand Designs* or in *Elle Decoration*, the retrosexual pad has its own definite look and themes. The following have all proved equally effective in pulling birds sick to death of blokes who've spent too long in Zara Home.

- **The Minimalist** – the loft space wankers would love this. 'You just don't notice the wardrobe space at all.' That's because there isn't any; his clothes are piled on the floor. He's got it down to a TV, a bed and fridge.
  What it says about you – *You're a get-out-and-enjoy-life kind of guy who might just be persuaded to watch TV in bed.*

- **The Practical Contemporary** – Similar to the minimalist except you have so many gadgets, video game devices, high-tech weapons and power tools that it looks cluttered.
  What it says about you – *You are unmistakably a bloke and have many interesting hobbies a girl could help you get rid of.*

- **Shabby Chic** – Your furniture juxtaposes a mix of styles to cleverly portray a cramped space, and the scuffs give it a certain rustic charm.
  What it says about you – *You seek answers, you're more concerned with the spiritual than the physical and you don't have the first fucking clue about furnishing a place.*

Blinds and curtains
Before squandering good beer money on soft furnishings, ask yourself whether you really need them. Let's face it – you're probably not going to be bothered to draw or close any curtains, and raising the blind is too much like hard work, so what's wrong with a carelessly-draped sheet to stop the nosey old biddy from number 25 peering in? There are times, though, when your money could be well spent. That bar of sunlight that seems to hit the TV only during big games needs shutting out, and if you can't get one of your lard-arse mates to stand in the way and block it out you'll need to take some kind of action.

Smaller spaces
Modern city living demands smaller and smaller dwellings, but there are ways in which you can make your flat seem bigger. Firstly, throw away anything wider than you which you can't cook with, sit on or watch. Secondly, don't invite anyone else in. You can always avoid feeling claustrophobic by going off to the pub.

Walls
Anything you put on the wall will be construed as making a statement, perhaps about your attitude to life, how you perceive the world, what art means to you etcetera. This is dangerous ground for a retrosexual and should be avoided at all times. Remember, even that Athena poster of the tennis player scratching her arse could ruin your chances of pulling.

Plants and Flowers
A well-positioned rubber plant or a bouquet of fresh flowers can add a freshness and brightness to an otherwise stilted room. A couple of days later, you'll have a wilting brown monstrosity or a few sticks lying in rapidly stagnating water. A plant pot will soon become an ash-tray and receptacle for dregs of tea and coffee, and the attendant very small and very irritating insects.

Lighting
A careful consideration of how you light different areas of your living space can help create the right mood for the occasion; on the other hand, a comprehensive arrangement of bare bulbs can send out just the right message about your ideas of home decor. They say that you're not here for long, could move out at any time and really couldn't give a toss.

Bathroom
First things first. It's your bathroom and if you want to leave the toilet seat up, you can. After all, how much effort does it really take to put it down again? For the retrosexual, to create the right image there are a few essential items you need for the smallest room. Try to have a few dog-eared lads' magazine lying somewhere around the toilet, some medicine or pills at least a year past the use-by-date and some free samples of aftershave you've stolen from magazines at the doctors. You should also attempt to clean the area on a regular basis. Once every few months – or when you can write your name in the grime in the bath – should be enough to show you're not a slob, but not some kind of hygiene freak.

Bedroom
This is where the action is going to happen. She needs to feel comfortable but know she's under pressure as the away side – a bit like going to Crystal Palace rather than Watford or Millwall. By all means change the sheets if there are too many crispy patches, but if by any chance there are no dirty socks and underpants littering the floor, try to spread a few around. After all, this is your bedroom not some scented Turkish boudoir. The line should, however, be drawn at displays of crunchy screwed up balls of tissue. You want her to think you are some kind of stud – not a cross between a teenager knuckle shuffler and a safari park chimp.

Garden
The retrosexual should have no qualms about gardening. Men have been pottering about in the garden long before Alan Titchmarsh became housewives' choice. Some describe the art of the gardener as being a constant battle to impose order on nature's insistent chaos, but given a taste of a few well-chosen power tools – a strimmer, a chainsaw or an angle-grinder – you'll find nature usually backs down for a while. A retrosexual treats his garden like Kissinger viewed small countries in the Far East – as experiments for decimation. You can't get Agent Orange down the garden centre, but you should be able to purchase enough chemicals to leave you with room to get your barbecue out on a showery summer Sunday.

Ten Things You Don't Need In The House

- Working doorbell: it'll only be the God Squad or someone collecting money.
- Cushions: just what are they for, exactly?
- Vases: like someone's going to turn up with flowers.
- Ornaments: as much use as tits on a nun.
- An espresso-maker: admit it, you never even worked out how to use it.
- Facial products: shaving foam is OK – no gel or oil, though.
- Candles: it's the 21st century – we've got electricity now.
- Dimmer switches: either on or off, it's that simple.
- Amusing magnetic characters which stick to the fridge.
- An answerphone: if it's that important, they'll ring back.

The Retrosexual In The Kitchen

No longer a woman's realm, the kitchen has been up for grabs for more than 20 years now. Men now feel obliged to be able to sauté, marinade and baste with the best of them and not ruin the pans. They are supposed to know the difference between fair trade, organic and slight mould and, even worse, are meant to give a toss. And, we still get moaned at for not doing the washing-up.

The truth is that more than half of the nation's men have blasted their tastebuds to kingdom come by misguidedly ordering the vindaloo at a late-night session at the local curry house – so much so that more than 80 percent wouldn't be able to tell the difference between parsley, sage and marijuana. And another whole bunch of them have the hygiene standards of arse-licking baboons. So do we really believe women want us in the kitchen, poncing around with an apron and spatula, crying, 'Darling, have you seen the nutmeg lately?'

Women are returning to the idea of a bloke who, having survived the era of nouvelle cuisine through an unhealthy intake of Guinness, is desperate for a large plateful of good grub. She is the one who will throw away anything approaching its consume-by date (he has a less scientific approach), she alone knows the value of defrosting before cooking, and she appreciates being able to create something he can devour in a couple of minutes.

Nobody wants to return to the dark, sexist days of 'Where's my dinner?' and, of course, it's right and proper for a man to prepare the odd meal for his lady. Just make sure she knows you're not interested in anything to do with food apart from eating it. For example, for all he cares the calorific values, ingredients, RDA vitamin percentages and fat content could be written in Chinese – although the picture of the serving suggestion can sometimes come in handy.

A woman invited to your flat could therefore well find herself inspecting your kitchen, and if she were to discover you possess such items as saffron, a garlic press or one of those blowtorches for making crème brûlée (for fuck's sake), it'd be as well to prepare a good excuse. If, like many women, she decides your performance in bed is inversely related to your performance in the kitchen, you could be in for another barren night.

Your kitchen or cooking space should be tidy (which shouldn't be difficult, considering you won't have much in it), but not sparkling. Remember, she needs to realize this is a room you barely know exists. You should own, and be able to operate, a working kettle, toaster, microwave and cooker (although the last is pretty optional). You might also possess a George Foreman grilling machine, a 1970s-style Breville sandwich-toaster or an impressive food processor or cappuccino-maker. These should be boxed, unopened and stashed away in the most inaccessible cupboard available.

Utensils should be kept to a bare minimum, namely a bottle-opener (that trick with your teeth is good, but as you get older the roots of your teeth become slacker and one day you'll be left with a bloody gap, teeth on the floor and – worst of all in that situation – a beer you can't open), a tin-opener, a saucepan and a large wok which can double up as a frying pan. Don't keep more than two plates and sets of knives and forks, or she might think you like to entertain.

The fridge-freezer is your real retrosexual badge of honour. On opening, it should be easy to judge your culinary skills. The first few shelves should be filled with beer (but it's surprising how few beers you can fit in a everyday fridge, so you might need to keep a box on top as well), but you will need room for other essentials such as a pint of milk, some 'I can't believe this stuff is butter', eggs and foil trays of leftover curry.

All this is not to imply that you never cook for yourself or that you go hungry. The retrosexual has an extensive repertoire of meals he is able to cook for himself – usually after a late night's drinking. Mainly these hark back to the days before fresh foodstuffs were readily available, before trustafarian drop-outs spent their weekends manning farmers' markets and before doctors became seriously concerned at the nation's cholesterol levels, but they will prove you have an interest in food that stretches only as far as your stomach.

Recipes For A Retrosexual

Cheesy beans

Place two slices of buttered (white, thick-sliced) bread on the worktop. Slice some cheddar cheese and cover each slice. Use your fist to gently create a hollow in the centre of the bread and spoon as many baked beans as you can into it. Now turn your toaster on its side and slot the bread in horizontally. When the cheese is bubbling, carefully remove the delicious snack. You should be careful to do this before the toaster 'pops up' as it can fire the snack right out and straight at your vulnerables. Serve with ketchup.

Curry

Fry whatever you might have – chicken, beef, leftover kebab – and add some supermarket curry sauce. It might not taste exactly like it does from a takeaway, but if you've had enough to drink you might not notice. Serve with ketchup.

Instant snack

It can be surprising how different flavours and textures can bring out the best in each other. In this case, a bag of cheese and onion crisps carefully mixed with a packet of dry roasted peanuts can deliver a whole new experience.

Eggy bread

Whisk four eggs with a splash of milk and some Worcester sauce. Soak thick slices of white bread in the egg mix and fry until a nice golden colour. Serve with ketchup.

Creamy crackers... er... microwaved

Spread some cheese on a cream cracker and microwave for five to ten seconds. Serve with ketchup.

Corned beef hash

Take a tin of baked beans, a tin of corned beef and a tin of new potatoes. Put the potatoes and beans in a pan and heat through. Cut the corned beef into large chunks and add to the pan. Season with spicy brown sauce and serve with ketchup.

Stir-fry

Make some rice or instant noodles and let them cool. Take whatever you have in the cupboard and put it all in a frying pan together. Add some chilli sauce or curry powder.

Crispy baked potato
Take a potato. Run it under the tap for a few seconds. Put oven on full and leave it there while you go to the pub. When you return, take it out of the oven and, using a hammer if necessary, chip away at the skin until you have a plateful of crispy bits. Serve with ketchup.

Rice pudding
When it's time for a dessert, there's nothing like a good rice pudding. Just reach to the back of the cupboard, blow the dust off and open the lid. Delicious if gently heated, but if you eat it cold out of the tin, it's not so bad and you save on the washing-up.

Tuna delight
Worried there's nothing in the cupboard for the little lady, should she ever pop round? Just keep a tin of tuna handy. God knows what you're meant to do with it, but women have a feel for these things and it'll make you seem Retrosexual and thoughtful at the same time.

The One Exception – A Barbeque

Like all good rules, there's an exception, and when the cooking takes place outdoors, our previously uninterested anti-gourmand becomes a *cordon bleu* chef complete with apron and a selection of cooking utensils. Just one sniff of burning charcoal and the sight of blood dripping from a steak sends the rotrosexual back to his caveman roots. As if to prove he knows all about cooking, but just can't be bothered with the indoors version, he carefully creates a back-garden Vesuvius by tossing the lighter fluid on to the coals, prizes salvageable parts of sausages from the grill and serves up another carbonized-on-the-outside, raw-on-the-inside chicken breast.

IT'S YOUR ROUND...

As the traditional pub is hounded into extinction by bars, gastropubs, and people who'd rather stay at home with cheap lager from the supermarket, retrosexuals are condemned to pound the streets like some kind of down-dressed bloodhound. Such is the parlous state of the nation's licensed properties that the search for a dingy, carpet-stained, male-dominated establishment can be a whole night's endeavour – but find one and you'll be transported back to a time when men could be men and women sat quietly with a half of lager and lime.

In all but the outermost reaches of the country, pubs have been transformed into either glorified youth clubs, wannabe restaurants or some kind of dance studio with polished floors and wall-to-ceiling mirrors. Alcopops, Sunday papers, quizzes and – God help us – karaoke have all been employed by the forces of darkness (aka marketing departments) to destroy the pub as we know it. Fortunately, they haven't succeeded, thanks to the unsung heroes of the nation who spend their time and money keeping the traditional boozer afloat. Quietly standing – sometimes swaying – at the bar, often for hours at a time, they are dedicated servants of the cause.

For the retrosexual, the pub is still a place of refuge, away from the girlfriend and the boss (a lot could be learned from the Mexicans, whose boozers still display signs saying 'No Women Or Uniformed Officers'). It's not a place for a business meeting, a five-course meal or a disco. OK, if a woman happens to venture all well and good, but this is your domain and never forget it.

So what makes a pub the kind of place a retrosexual can feel at home? As soon as you enter, you're welcomed by the musty smell of stale beer and drying clothes. The only things on the bar are soiled bar towels and a 1970s collection box with a model of a boy in calipers. The surly, and definitely not antipodean, bar staff manage to serve you before chatting incessantly to their mates and they don't slop the top inch off the pint when they pass it to you (that's 80p's-worth in some places). And, just to get the ambience right, the salted peanuts reveal ever more of the bikini-clad model as they are purchased.

Does it need to be friendly? It's never great when everyone turns round and stares at you when you walk in, and it's useful to be on nodding terms with a few of the regulars. You never know when it might come in handy if you need a plumber, there's a hot plasma TV for sale or it all goes off on a Friday night.

Know the landlord or landlady by name? No. They're doing a job and you shouldn't mistake professionalism for a heartfelt desire to hear your latest anecdote. You might think you're salt-of-the-earth, all-things-to-all-men, hail-fellow-well-met, but when you call out 'Another pint of your frothy deliciousness, Trevor,' the rest of the pub will be sharing but one thought – 'Twat.'

Pub Names

In this golden age of marketing, pub names are the subject of brewery marketeers' meetings. They are eager to appeal to the right demographic. ('Demographic' means a group of people who have nothing whatsoever in common with you.) A real pub name should have history and gravity, and not sound like it was invented by a bloke with over-long sideburns at a wipe board. Any place which has a 'something and' (such as the Halibut and iPod or Parrot and Bungee) should therefore be avoided at all costs. Try to stick to pubs with two words in their name and one of them should be 'The'. The Anchor, The Wheatsheaf, The Bull etcetera won't guarantee you a decent boozer, but it might cut down your chances of encountering people actually buying champagne at the bar.

Music

Retrosexuals aren't killjoys – they like a bit of Nelly Furtado as much as the next man – but there's a time, a place and a volume. A good pub has a jukebox with hits from across the decades, which are played at a level where you're never completely sure whether the track you put on has actually played or not. And, while there may be the occasional disco upstairs after hours on a Friday night, there's never a need for a DJ in the bar area pumping out beats so loud that you can't hear yourself think (if you were the kind of bloke who thought anything of thinking).

Food

Retrosexuals go to pubs to drink, not eat, yet as pub after pub fancies itself as a Jamie Oliver-style eaterie, you're likely to encounter the landlord welcoming you with something like, 'How about trying our homemade loin of rare Gloucester spotted boar with pan-fried scallops and mash?' and you'll find him pretty unimpressed with your request for a packet of pork scratchings. Yes, pubs *should* do food: crisps, nuts (even the dry-roasted which no one has actually tasted since 1982), Mini Cheddars, the aforementioned unimaginable-which-bit-of-pig-they-used pork snack and a large jar of pickled onions on the bar. Doorstep sandwiches (ham, cheese or ham and cheese) can be served at lunchtime, and every now and then the landlord may introduce a hot evening meal – usually a hotpot – which is taken off the menu after an unsuccessful couple of weeks.

Big Screen

The sign 'Sport Screened Here' is a ubiquitous sight outside the boozers of the land, and, sad though it sometimes is to see the nation's manhood straining to see whether Boston United can peg back Weymouth's first-half strike, the truth is that football has helped keep the pub a blokes' zone. Blokes can easily sit in silence together for 90 minutes and extra time if necessary – only resorting to the occasional grunt of 'Studs up, that' or 'Kinnel, Tommy!' Incredibly popular though football is – and big games will see all the plonkers and their girlfriends turn out – it takes a certain devotion to your retrosexual values to sit through a miserable 0-0 draw between two underachieving Midlands teams on a wet Monday night. And to those still unconvinced, I say cast your mind back, if you can, to the Big Screen's predecessor – the video jukebox. Case closed.

Indoor Sports

Real pub games don't interfere with a bloke trying to get his head round the day's racing, they don't find you being jostled by groups of students as they try to think up a crazy team name and they don't feature some tuneless dimmock who fancies himself as the new Mick Hucknall (as if one wasn't enough). Pool, darts, table football, West Country bowling alleys and – this is to show that being retrosexual isn't necessary the same as being an old fart – even video games are fine traditional bar-room activities, but whoever invented the pub quiz needs to be hung by the bollocks. They attract beardy, *Guardian*-reading know-it-alls, fill the pub with people willing to stab each other for the free round that is the grand winning prize and involve the landlord, who already has the most tedious voice in Christendom, using a PA.

PUB ETIQUETTE

Is there really any need for this? Unfortunately, judging from the lads and metros hogging the sofas or trying to attract the waiter's attention or burying themselves in the serious Sunday papers (especially those biting the ends of their biros as they set about the crossword), the need has never been greater.

- A retrosexual always stands at the bar – even if he has recently lost both kneecaps and there is no one else in the pub.
- A retrosexual will always pay for his drinks with cash and will look in complete distaste at anyone proffering a credit card.
- An arriving retrosexual will always buy a pint for any of his mates already in the pub, even if they have just bought a full pint and have to leave in the next couple of minutes.
- A retrosexual is permitted to drink the following beverages: beer, lager, whisky, vodka and a Bailey's if someone has left it unfinished on the bar.
- A retrosexual will never drink from a half-pint glass.
- A retrosexual will not let a woman order drinks (although he is allowed to accept the money), nor will he buy her a pint. She drinks white wine or a half of lager and lime.
- A retrosexual always buys a pint (and, often, a whisky chaser) at the first sounding of last orders – whatever the circumstances.
- A retrosexual does not read a book or newspaper (with the possible exception of the racing pages) at the bar. If not engaged in conversation, he surveys the state of the optics, stares at the barmaid's arse or jangles his change in his pocket.
- A retrosexual will refuse ice, lemon or any other fruit in his spirits and will rip away any lime tucked into the neck of a beer bottle.
- A retrosexual catches the barperson's eye with a glance or a nod. He does not flap his tenner or twenty about like a performing seal.

TAKING THE PISS – URINAL ETIQUETTE

This chapter really shouldn't be necessary. You'd think it's common sense, but wander into any public convenience these days and you'll see all sorts – blokes on their own just hanging around, blokes going in the cubicles in pairs;– it's like a breath of fresh air when you go in and someone's just having a piss. They might not teach this stuff at school, but if you're going to survive as a retrosexual, it's a code of conduct you need to know.

General Rules

You're on your own. Women might enjoy the camaraderie, gossip and security of going to the loo together. That's fine. Men don't. On no occasion should you and a friend share a visit to the porcelain park. People will leap to all kinds of conclusions, there is nothing to be gained and it's wrong: just plain wrong.

Man on a mission. You are going to the lavvy for one reason and one reason only. Go directly there, do what you have to do and come back. Don't become interested in the interesting varieties of fruit condoms available, the advert for the moped service that gets you and your car home or the interesting plumbing solutions employed. Just get yourself out of there as soon as possible.

Eyes down. From the moment you enter the convenience (or rest room – as if all you're after is a rest, as our American cousins call it), you must avoid making eye contact with anyone. Stare directly at the wall or keep your gaze in a downward direction, even if the overflowing urinal sounds like Niagara.

Shut the fuck up. This is no place to start your male bonding. If you're that desperate for a conversation, ring the Samaritans. Some hardline retrosexuals insist on total silence in the john, but we should allow for the more relaxed modern times. I witnessed a novice returning from a trip last week with a bloody nose. When I asked if he had made the cardinal mistake of striking up a conversation, he replied, 'I only said, "I didn't know you were Jewish."' However, the following vocabulary is deemed acceptable: 'All right, mate?' if you see someone you know (anyone in this situation is automatically referred to as 'mate'), 'After you, mate' to proffer a vacant urinal to someone, 'Cheers, mate' if someone allows you to go first, or 'Fuck off' if they say anything else (you can dispense with the 'mate' appendage in this case).

No funny stuff. Once you're inside the gents, it's essential you make no unexpected movements. Don't stop to do your shoelaces up, swap urinals mid-piss or go to the mirror and start rearranging your hair. Most importantly here, you only need to undo your flies and get the old chap out. What are these people doing rummaging around for five minutes or undoing their belt and trouser buttons and then the flies? Holy shit.

Using The Cubicle

Entering the cubicle in a public convenience is a brave step. Once you're in, you can't retreat until you've completed your business, no matter what disgusting state it's in. To do so is to lose considerable face. There are only two reasons you will use the cubicle: firstly, and obviously, if you desperately need a dump; secondly, if – under the rules stated below – there is no urinal available. In the latter case, it is essential that you leave the door fully open.

The Engaged Urinal Problem

A single urinal presents few problems unless you enter the area to find someone else is using it. Try to avoid this situation by keeping one eye on the bog before you make your move and, if you know another bloke's in the toilet, just wait until he returns. If the situation's unavoidable, immediately turn your back to the pisser and turn your attention to washing your hands in a meticulous manner. If it's a cramped area, use this time to think carefully about how you're going to negotiate the changeover.

Urinal Choice

How's your maths? Because if it doesn't come naturally, you're going to have to work hard to master this. The basic rule is that you should always leave a buffer urinal between you and the next man. So far, so easy, but what if there's no one there? What if more than one urinal is being used? What if there's a choice of two buffers? The following table should provide some help. Imagine a pub toilet with six urinals. We'll call them U1, U2, U3, U4, U5, U6. We could therefore face the following situations:

1. None of the urinals are in use. *Choose U1 – the urinal closest to the door.*

2. U1 only is in use. *Choose U6 – the furthest urinal from the one in use.*

3. U1 and U6 are both in use. *There is no middle urinal in this scenario, so you are compelled to choose between U3 and U4 and make a snap judgement based on pissing style, how threatening they look and their likely sexual preference.*

4. U1, U4 and U6 are all in use. *Here you are forced to stand next to someone. U5 would mean you are directly between two others, leaving either U2 or U3 to be chosen depending on the least likely neighbour to spray your shoes.*

Farting

The retrosexual likes to be thought of as a decent chap, but who can't help but let one out at the end of a good piss? For this reason it's acceptable to let rip in a public toilet, but only while you're actually at the urinal. And it's not about showing off. Do what's necessary, and make sure it's just a Southern breeze and doesn't follow through to a brown frown.

The Hippy Happy Shake

When does a quick shake of the old fella to dispose of the last drops become a serious case of bashing the bishop? There are no hard-and-fast rules, but the consensus seems to be that four or five shakes should suffice. Six or seven tugs look suspicious, nine or ten yanks constitute self-abuse and more than 12 should be grounds for an arrest (especially if the person involved hasn't even urinated). And, whatever you do, don't look at it until it's time to put it away.

Hand Wash

A retrosexual always washes his hands after visiting the toilet; it's common decency and separates him from the scumbags. It is not, however, completely necessary to dry them afterwards, especially if there's just a hot-air dryer which will involve you spending even more time behind the toilet door. A quick wipe on the arse of your jeans is usually enough.

GETTING ABOUT

The retrosexual is a proud man, and never more so than when he's out and about. He knows where he's going and how to get there – and if he doesn't know, he bloody well pretends he does. As much as they may openly mock man's seemingly illogical but steely resolution, women secretly love the inner strength of refusing to admit you're wrong.

At the heart of being a retrosexual is not knowing where the fuck you're going, but marching or driving on nevertheless. He's never lost; he just hasn't got there yet, and would as soon ask a stranger for directions as wear a badge saying, 'I've a tiny penis and I like *Antiques Roadshow*.' Better men than you have spent days striding along streets in search of some familiar landmark to get them back on course; Captain Scott might even have been first to the South Pole if he hadn't been too proud to ask someone. Furthermore, if ever you're offered help by a busybody passer-by, you must reject their aid with an irritated and barely polite utterance of, 'It's OK, I know where I am.'

In the car, there can be no greater humiliation than having to wind down the window to admit to a complete stranger that you barely deserve the name of a man. It's a primeval instinct; trust no one when you're on the hunt. It's a dog-eat-dog world and they might mislead you in an attempt to get there first, even if you're only on the way to the late-night shop for a pint of milk.

You Need Wheels

Generally speaking, proper men still drive cars, but in these days of global warming, clogged roads and congestion charges, they can be forgiven for seeking out other means of transport that don't make them look complete tits. Motorbikes are an obvious alternative; you get to ride a powerful machine and wear leathers without posing.

None of this, however, applies to any machine below 150cc, especially the whining little mopeds or scooters that clog up the nation's roads and car parks. You might think it's just the thing for the busy modern man, but in truth you just look like a 16-year-old who's finally graduated from racing round the council estate.

Cycling is also an increasingly popular means of getting about town: cheap and relatively quick, good for your fitness, but guaranteed to have you arriving at your destination sweating, red-faced and out of control, like one of those wobbly blokes at the end of the marathon. If that isn't enough to blow your pulling power, you could always try dressing from head to toe in flab-revealing lycra and embellishing it with a luminous jacket and ridiculous helmet that marks you out as a wuss who's patently scared of roads full of psychopaths driving juggernauts.

If you're going to cycle with retrosexual appeal, the only way is on an old sit-up-and-beg bike, never going so fast that you're out of breath, but fast enough to keep ahead of little old ladies with baskets. Never wear a helmet or use lights and casually sail through every red light, pedestrian crossing and junction. If you survive long enough, you could still look like a reasonably cool bloke – for someone who hasn't got a car.

And, so to public transport. Firstly, forget the bus. The only retrosexual you'll ever find on a bus is the driver. Buses are for schoolkids, old-age pensioners and knife-carrying care-in-the-community cases. And, while the train's more acceptable, it's often more of a nightmare. Getting on rush-hour underground trains is like a cock being forced into a condom: it's tricky getting on, it can never quite feel comfortable and you emerge looking a right mess.

'In 150 Metres Turn Left At The Next Junction – You Muppet.'

Satellite navigation systems sem to have caught the public imagination and are now even seemingly within the reach of people who were previously unable to afford a decent road map. A marvellous technological leap, I'm sure we'd all agree, but there is a downside: the loss of the main conversational gambit open to an ordinary chap. Men were born with a precise knowledge of how to get to anywhere and back again without paying a toll, getting stuck in a traffic jam or missing out on a stretch of motorway where there are never any traffic cops.

Every lad has sat in admiration of his father discussing with his mates the routes to places they had no intention of ever visiting. 'I'd take the M3 to junction 16, the A32 as far as that pub with the wonky chimney, then you can double back on yourself, cross over the by-pass and...' 'Bollocks', his mate would reply. 'You want the M4 to junction 7, the B4147 and then if you take the track through the sewage works, you can get on to the road that hasn't even got a number yet because we only finished building it on Friday.' Golden memories, lost to a generation now forced to argue with a small box on the dashboard.

Of course, it could soon be possible to buy a retrosexual sat nav. This transcript stolen from system trials gives an idea of how it might sound:

'You know you've got to turn right up here, don't you?'
'Past the bookies and that pub with the tasty barmaid then it's left.'
'Left, you muppet. Don't you ever fucking listen?'
'You gonna hoot at this bird with the mini-skirt?'
'Ha! What a minger! Bet you feel a right prat now!'
'Sorry, I fell asleep. Where are we?'
'Stop in 50 metres at the Green Man. I'm dying for a pint.'

THE NOT-SO-LITTLE HORROR OF SHOPS

Therapy. The very word makes one's toes curl and sends a shiver through your whole being. But for all the hippy, New Age-y bollocks of aromatherapy, reflexology and shih tsu shiatsu (a small dog runs up and down your back), the one therapy that can turn a retrosexual into one big raging Y chromosome is retail therapy – the art of shopping to make you feel better.

That's right, for some people (you know whom I mean by now), trudging round an airless shopping centre, looking at stuff they can't afford, trying on clothes they have no intention of buying and, eventually, paying out good money for something they don't need, is considered fun. Shopping has ceased to be an irritating necessity of life and has transformed into a leisure occupation.

Christmas Shopping

The shops might get their decorations up in October, your girlfriend keeps telling you how many shopping days there are until Christmas and your mum's given you her present list weeks ago, but the true retrosexual will never do his Christmas shopping until Christmas Eve, between 5pm and 6pm. Half-pissed, he will indulge in the traditional scurrying in and out of shops in desperation, spending far too long looking at lingerie, before purchasing something completely inappropriate or costing twice as much as he intended to spend because he just can't face it any more. Alternatively, he just buys the same thing as last year and the year before: perfume for the girlfriend, chocolates for his mum and a home brew kit for his dad. His brother doesn't get anything because the bastard didn't bother getting anything for him last year.

Supermarket Shopping

A retrosexual treats every trip to the supermarket as if he's on one of those gameshows to collect as much as he can in two minutes. He knows what he wants, the quickest way to it and instinctively finds the shortest till queue. He's the bloke everyone wants to be behind in the queue: he packs quickly, has no reward cards or vouchers and pays with cash. And, if his milk is leaking or a can of beans is dented, he doesn't wait for half an hour until someone can be bothered to get him another; he puts it aside and says, 'Sod it, I'll get it next time.' These are the men you sometimes see out shopping with their partners, inwardly groaning at having to slowly track down every aisle, raising their eyes to the heavens as she endlessly compares prices and grimacing as they waltz straight past the drinks section.

'I Need Your Opinion'

She needs you. What better way to appeal to the retrosexual than to flatter his independent mind? Don't fall for it. Tear your legs off to bloody stumps rather than enter a women's clothes shop with her. There, time is measured differently. Hours can pass on one rail of clothes. Then she goes to try them on, which leaves you looking like a perv hanging around the changing area just so you can say, 'I like that, I really do', which is pointless because no matter how many times you say it, she's never going to believe you.

An Acceptable Side Of Shopping?

There are some shops a retrosexual can be seen in and still maintain his dignity. Fishing and hunting shops carry considerable interest, hours can be whiled away in a large bookshop (often spent looking for the third title in a 'buy two and get the third free' offer) and electrical appliance stores are sometimes worth a wander, even if it's just to catch the football results on a Saturday afternoon. Hobby shops, however, remain in the balance. What self-respecting man can't show some interest in a 1:250 scale model of a battleship or the latest copy of *Deathmonger* comic, but if you're discovered hanging around these kinds of establishments for too long, you've crossed the border into Nerdville – a land where no woman will ever tread.

Ten Shopping Expeditions To Avoid

'We never do anything together any more,' she'll whine and she's not talking about going for a curry in the afternoon, taking you to a bare knuckle boxing match or joining a swingers group. It means there is a shopping trip in the offing. Stand proud; one of the following is probably what she has in mind...

- **The out-of-town experience** – an electrical goods chainstore, a big chemist, a 'sports' shop selling cheap, nasty clothes made by five-year-olds in China and a drive-in burger joint. Oh, Mama! Hold me back!

- **Saturday afternoon, city centre** – God save us from pedestrianization: the over-excited adolescents abusing each other in what passes these days for flirting, the procession of wheelchairs, prams and motorized old people, the clipboard-wielding chuggers at every corner, hundreds of cafes all smelling of wet clothes. And no pubs.

- **The shopping mall** – your feet ache, you're convinced the exit is just around the corner, you're sure you've been in John Lewis seven times already, you've been here four bloody hours already. Then you discover there are still three more floors of this hell.

- **Scandinavian-style furniture stores** – how much are you prepared to put up with for a decent plate of meatballs in the restaurant? The eight-mile walk from the car park, being rammed by someone with a flat-pack cupboard they've overloaded on their unwieldy trolley, the eight-hour queue for the tills or the chance your names will be added to the relationships that sadly met their end at this spot.

- **The let's-smarten-you-up trip** – the most excruciating, humiliating and embarrassing experience known to man is being escorted by a woman into a blokes' clothes shop. Unsuitable items will be held up against you, she will ask the shop assistant questions, you'll end up with armfuls of things to try on and be forced to emerge from the cubicle to parade them. You might go in a man, but you'll come out a eunuchpot.

- **The carpet store** – there's just carpets, and more carpets – oh, and great, some laminate flooring.

The Shopping Retrosexual Overheard

'Yep, that looks nice, get that. Then we can go.'

'Is it time for a drink yet?'

'I'm not unhappy, it's just that the wanton consumerism makes me feel physically sick.'

'There's a great black-and-white film on this afternoon.'

'I'm not asking him, he's 14, is wearing white socks and can't see past his exploding acne.'

'This would be a prime spot for a terrorist bomb.'

'It's another fiver at the car park if we don't go now.'

'I think I've just lost the will to live.'

'But where are we going to put it?'

'No. We're just browsing.'

WHERE'S YOUR TABLE MANNERS?

You could go your whole life without facing the dilemmas posed by a restaurant and your problems would be confined to whether 'You want fries with that?', exactly what kind of animal your local fried chicken emporium has dipped in breadcrumbs, and whether to go for the saveloy or the minced beef and onion pie.

So why would you want go to a restaurant? These are such feminine places, thoughtfully planned, decorated with an exquisite aesthetic touch and carefully lit. Women love them and feel part of them, whereas a man would never want to live in one; they only go because women force them to or because the alternative is cooking.

Choosing The Restaurant

Deciding where you are going to eat is your first dilemma. Your choice will obviously be a takeaway or a stool in the window of the KFC, but just face it: sooner or later, your bird is going expect to be wined and dined or you might find you lose your special extras. However, this is your only concession. Any more and you're going to look soft or, even worse, like you're enjoying it. You don't spend days researching restaurant reviews on the internet; you don't ring up and book a table – they're only going to ask intrusive questions such as 'What's your name?' or 'For what time do you want the table?'.Just ask a mate where he went and turn up. If it's fully booked, suggest a takeaway or a KFC; you tried.

The Pre-Meal Ordeal

The formalities of dining out have been designed to intimidate even the toughest of men. Be prepared. Your objective is to face humiliation with dignity and not to storm out in temper.

- In certain establishments you might encounter some spotty herbert who wants to park the car for you. Unaccustomed as you will be to giving your keys to anaemic teenagers, for the good of the date try to hand them over without a threat of what you'll do to his bollocks if there's so much as a scratch on your pride and joy.
- Your table isn't going to be ready. Let them know you've arrived and head straight for the bar area. This could be your last chance of getting a beer for hours.
- When you approach your table, quickly put your coat on the back of the seat, sit down and take the napkin off the table. Hesitate and you'll find some smarmy waiter taking your coat to God knows where, pulling the chair out for you and placing the napkin on your lap (with his hands in a proximity to your privates reserved for the doctors at the STD clinic).

The Drinks Menu

There's no point starting to moan that there are no mini kievs on the menu you're given; it's probably the wine list. Calm down. No one actually chooses any of them; they're just there to show off what a great selection they have. Ask for the house red and close the menu. Fizzy or still water? However it comes from the tap.

The Menu

Once you have the menu in your hand, you have the power. Now you can begin to display the confidence, decisiveness and authority that mark out the retrosexual. Look down the menu and see how many dishes you understand and how many you can pronounce without embarrassment. At this point you need to make sure the waiter knows what you're about by asking a leading question, such as:

* How long is it going to take?
* Does that come with chips – err, French fries?
* Can you bring some ketchup with it?
* Which steak is the one that covers the whole plate?
* Does the fish have a head on it?
* I'd like the Thai beef, but not with the noodles, with the vegetables from the roast chicken instead.

On the other hand, questions such as those listed below imply you are a fish out of water, a quivering blob of jelly just lining up for ritual humiliation.

* Is the chicken organic? (No, it's dead!)
* What would you recommend? (Because I don't have a mind of my own.)
* What's the soup of the day? (Yeah, like you were really going to order it.)
* Is the fish farmed or wild? (As if you, who are used to eating half-defrosted fish fingers, are going to be able to taste the difference.)
* Is the duck à l'orange (or whatever) good? (What do you expect them to say? 'No, Sir. Well done. It's fucking awful. We only put it on the menu to catch out idiots, which you clearly are not.')

And one more thing. Don't trust the 'specials' written in a down-home kind of way on a blackboard. If they're that special, why aren't they on the menu? It's always possible they're just getting rid of their leftovers.

The Cutlery And Other Conundrums

Now you have a precious few moments in which to ponder your place setting. Before you could be a confusing array of glasses, knives, forks, plates, bread, the beer bottle you brought in from the bar and your mobile phone. There are established positions for all of these, but you're never going to remember, so don't let it concern you.

More worrying is the arrival of implements and gear with which you're not familiar: chopsticks, fish knives, crab hammers, even bibs can materialize at the table if you haven't ordered with care. If this looks like happening, the only sensible thing to do is grab a knife and fork, and hang on to them for dear life, slipping them (delicately) under your napkin if necessary.

The safest option of all is to order food you can eat with your hands. You'll be surprised how sexy some women find watching a man peel a prawn, tear a crab's leg apart or nibble on a corn on the cob (perhaps), at least in comparison to slurping and spilling your soup.

Enjoy Your Meal, Sir

The gap between giving your order to the waiter and the subsequent arrival of food is designated conversation time for you and your companion. For the metrosexual, this can be a delicate period when he chooses to discuss the ambiance, décor or clientèle of the restaurant. Fortunately, for you there are no such worries. A simple glance around, a nod and a quiet 'Nice gaff' will be enough. Your date will, no doubt, then begin to talk expansively about everything and anything. Your task here is quite straightforward: all you have do is listen and wonder just how long it takes to fry a bit of steak.

If your meal arrives but your companion food is delayed, it's polite not to tuck in immediately. Count to five, look her in the eyes, look round to see if the waiter's coming back and if he isn't, then you can start. Of course, if she's sitting with a full plate and you're still staring at the crumbs of your bread roll, it's perfectly fine to pick at her chips.

When you have both received your meals, the retrosexual on a first date has a golden opportunity to display his ability to take control of the situation. Complain. There are a million things that can be wrong: the food is too hot, too cold, overcooked, undercooked... It's simple: discreetly call the waiter over and, without raising your voice, let him know something is amiss.

The Bill

Your next major hurdle will be getting out of the place as quickly as you can. The waiter has you settled comfortably and has better things to do than rush around so that you can get back in time for *Match Of The Day*, and you have more dignity than to do that pathetic pretend-scribbling-on-your-hand thing, so between the two of you there needs to be a compromise. This may be reached in the following ways:

- Raising the index finger and, when you catch his eye, giving a slight nod.
- Dropping a gentler hint, such as standing up, stretching and putting your coat on.
- Walking over to the waiter, grabbing the lapels of his waistcoat and telling him if he doesn't sort the bill out immediately you'll shove what's left of your lobster right up his Terrine de Foies de Volaille.

The retrosexual will always settle his bill with cash, but there's still the problem of tipping. The commonly accepted figure in the UK is 15 per cent, but this can be pretty difficult to work out after two beers, a bottle of wine, a large whisky and both the complimentary sambucas. Basically, you're paying the bloke again just for doing his job because the restaurant can't stretch to paying him the minimum wage. Your choice here is simple: flash the cash to show how generous – and, even better, magnanimous, if he's been crap – you are or leave nothing at all ('You want a tip? Start a trade union.') Whatever you do, don't start an appraisal process – 'We'll start at 15 per cent, take off three per cent for sneering at the request for brown sauce, add two per cent for agreeing to turn the Amy Winehouse CD off...'). You need to get out of that place as quickly as possible and with your dignity only slightly dented.

THE RETROSEXUAL ABROAD

Once you have perfected your retrosexual persona at home, you might be tempted to try your luck abroad. Beware! Though the British invented most of the good things in life – football, apple crumble, punk rock, pornography – Johnny Foreigner has never felt the need to be 'retro' sexual. Throughout the Mediterranean nations, unless you have three mistresses and your wife spends all day cleaning their houses as well as your own, you will come across as some kind of lily-livered castrato.

The retrosexual abroad must try to be open to the different cultures and the sometimes surprising ways of life he might encounter. For example, moustaches are rife in Turkey and it would be foolish to assume that everyone sporting a 'Freddie Mercury' is either gay or hiding a unfortunate cold sore. In Italy, you might spot many men carry handbags on their evening promenade. There's usually a good reason for this and, besides, not all of them contain make-up. And, out and about in Paris, you may notice that a Frenchman can sit for hours over one small glass of pastis. There's not necessarily anything wrong with them; French people can get drunk on much less than us.

The main thing you will need to assimilate once you leave your home is the different attitude to the body. Women on the continent are much less inhibited and are much more likely to get their kit off. In Munich, office workers spend their summer lunch breaks sunbathing nude in the park. All along the Mediterranean, there are beautiful topless girls sunning themselves and from Sweden to Slovakia advertising billboards show models with magnificent lathered-up breasts. In general, you're pretty lucky to turn around and not get an eyeful, so you'll have to work hard to keep yourself in hand and make use of their poor standards of plumbing by taking the odd cold shower.

There is also a refreshingly honest attitude to prostitution. Many countries' enlightened policies recognize that a man will quite often get so desperate for sex that he's quite willing to pay good money for time with an emaciated Dutch heroin addict, a Vietnamese ladyboy or a 19-stone peasant grandmother willing to raise her hundredweight of skirts in your direction. Also, in many places on the continent you can just walk into a legalized brothel. This is worth knowing, because you might stray into a bar and assume the local girls are sick of their moped-driving, smart-casual boys and that your chirpy British nature is just what they've been waiting for.

All this is, of course, pretty irrelevant, because the chances are that you won't even get out of Ayia Napa, or Faliraki, or whatever picturesque resort you're in. These are perfect training camps for the young retrosexual overseas and allow you to assimilate gently into a continental situation, getting to grips with local customs while remaining in the comfort zone of your culture. During your time here, it is important to:

- Avoid any local cuisine and survive purely on fish and chips, kebabs and full English breakfasts.
- Always go out bare-chested, except on formal occasions, when you may wear your football shirt.
- Show the locals that you will not be intimidated by their freakish weather by aiming to get a tan – somewhere between lobster and London bus red – by day two.
- Always avoid speaking any foreign language (except for their word for 'beer', which you may need to repeatedly shout at them if they don't understand their own language delivered in an Estuary slur).
- Take your own stock of brown sauce and teabags.

By taking these steps, holidaying British women at least will recognize your independence of thought and admire the way you've toned down your normal behaviour out of respect for your hosts. They'll also be completely bladdered most of the time and happy to tell you which dismal Northern city they hail from, by way of a chat-up line. Thereafter, sex is normally freely available to those still able to stand up after 12.30am.

5. LIVING MORE OF THE RETROSEXUAL LIFE

A MAN'S BEST FRIEND?

Men like animals – and I don't just mean fried or roasted. They recognize a common sense of independence, they admire their struggle to survive, they empathize with the constant search for food and they share a desire to shag any member of the opposite sex whenever the opportunity arises. All well and good, but do you want them in your house? And what does having a pet say about the retrosexual?

Cats are sinister, selfish and incredibly irritating when they do that circling thing around your legs – and certain women love them. They treat them like babies, refuse to leave them to go away for a weekend and give them the physical attention they'll deny to you. There's no better 'Keep out' sign than a single woman with a cat.

So why would a single man have a cat? Not for company; like a teenage son, they wolf down their tea and are off for the night fighting and screwing. Not for protection; that look is oh-so-evil, but not half as damaging as a well-placed size nine. And certainly not for fun; 'playing' with Moggie leaves you with gangrenous scratchmarks down your forearms. So all the stinking cat trays and disgusting food are just to make you look caring and sensitive. According to a Cats Protection League survey, 90 per cent of single women surveyed thought men who like cats are 'nicer' than men who don't – and now we're in the 21st century, we all realize 'nice' is just a euphemism for 'don't want to sleep with'.

On the other hand, a man can have a special understanding with his dog. This is a pet which can be a companion when you need one, will happily sit in the corner waiting for you to be in a better mood and can make you look hard when you're out walking with them. Some men might even claim they're better off living with a dog than a woman. After all, a dog's time in the bathroom is confined to a quick drink. They don't expect you to call when you're running late – the later you are, the more excited dogs are to see you. You never have to wait for a dog, they're instantly ready to go out. And they find you amusing and fun when you're drunk.

For women, the sight of a man and his dog is a romantic sight. Just like his bond with football, they suspect it's a relationship they can never have, yet it's so temptingly close. He shows that, at one and the same time, he can be protective, understanding, fun and loving – and still notice if it's had a haircut. Cruelly, some women maintain that the reason a man can co-exist so easily with his dog is because they share the same characteristics:

- They like to spend all day sprawled on the most comfortable piece of furniture.
- They shamelessly fart at will.
- They share irrational fears about vacuum-cleaning.
- They both have an inordinate fascination with women's crotches.
- They can hear a packet of biscuits being opened half a mile away, but can't hear a woman in the same room.
- Neither knows how to talk on the telephone.

ART AND CULTURE

Paintings, books, film, theatre and music, we're told in all earnestness, are the bedrock of civilization. They claim that without the *Mona Lisa* (minging bird with a grump on), James Joyce's *Ulysses* (500 pages of meaningless, garbled nonsense) and Beethoven's Fifth Symphony (da-da-da-dum and another three and a half hours) we would be somehow a lesser species. Now, we all like a dance and a movie now and then – but if you had to give something up, what would it be? Stella or Shakespeare? Cheese and onion crisps or Tchaikovsky? Fellatio or Fellini? Exactly.

Congratulations. As a retrosexual, you will no longer have to spend your Sunday mornings traipsing around hangover-punishing white-walled art galleries trying to work out if the fire extinguisher is a cleverly ironic installation or just a fire extinguisher. Saturday afternoons won't find you tiring of reading the subtitles on the latest French art-house movie and wondering what the football scores are, and you'll never find yourself finishing the latest Booker Prize winner at 3am and wondering what the fuck it was all about and whether it actually has ended or whether there are pages missing.

This isn't to say that the retrosexual's mind is an empty shell devoid of interest in the world of culture. Today's women won't be surprised to see you with a book or at the cinema, but only on your own terms. Gone are the days when she'll be impressed by your (fake) giggling as you read her copy of *Bridget Jones' Diary* or be turned on by your broadmindedness when she spots you in the queue for *Brokeback Mountain;* instead, she'll be intrigued and admiring of your own choice of cultural pursuits

Art

They're a clever lot, these artists, and they'll try all kinds of tricks to get blokes into a gallery. Nowadays, you can't venture out without coming across an exhibition of dead sheep in aspic, photos of guitar-toting rock stars, discarded knickers on a bed and live human dissections. Curious though it might be to watch someone with a beard laughing at a Gilbert and George piece, the best way to take in such galleries is to stroll purposefully through to the cafe, pausing only briefly to confirm that there's absolutely nothing you could possibly want in the shop.

Literature

There's little arguing with Mark Twain's famous quote that 'The man who doesn't read good books has no advantage over the man who can't read them.' However, he failed to mention the bloke who does read occasionally, when he can remember where he put the book and what page he was on, and takes a year and a half to finish a paperback. While never a prolific reader, the retrosexual does like to have a book on the go, usually one of the following:

- Any book by Andy McNab about how 'I was in the SAS once, honest, although I can't officially tell you that.'
- A Mafia-related biography, usually of a 'made guy' called Jimmy the Something.
- An autobiography of a sportsman who tragically but amusingly wasted his talents by devoting his life to women, drinking and gambling.
- Car manuals.

Theatre

No way. No. It's not right. They're just in front of you, pretending to be someone else. Let's not be ridiculous here.

Film

At last, a medium any self-respecting man can enjoy. Movies have always allowed men to escape their humdrum lives and wallow in their deepest fantasies, such as blowing up huge buildings, being completely outnumbered by murderous assassins but emerging victorious and unscathed, outwitting cruel guards to escape incarceration and rogering Faye Dunaway senseless on the kitchen table. Really classy films manage at least two of the above and throw in some gratuitous, gory violence too. Unfortunately, Hollywood's recent concentration on teen and chick flicks have driven men in search of fights and explosions back to the DVD shop: and, when your girlfriend turns up from late-night shopping to find you relaxing in your armchair with a bottle of beer watching one of the following, your retrosexual points will hit the roof.

The Western

This is man stripped down to his basic self – a kind of football player with chaps – relying on just a horse, a gun and his cowboy hat to get by in life. His choice is always stark and simple: do the right thing even if it means the barber, the bartender and most of the inhabitants of the two-dimensional shop fronts that pass for a frontier town are gunned down in the final battle.

- **Top selection:** *High Noon*, *The Magnificent Seven*, *The Good, The Bad and The Ugly*.
- **Retrosexual values:** the struggle for survival in a dog-eat-dog world – and plenty of beans.

The War Film

World War II wasn't won by Americans, Winston Churchill or the invention of radar; it was thanks to chaps with names like Ginger, Taffy and Tug taking over Düsseldorf, but managing to fly back to Blighty with only one wing, or the fellows at Stalag XIV determined to outwit their Nazi captors using only a cracked shaving mirror, some boot polish and a fake Belgian guestworker's passport.

- **Top selection:** *Paths Of Glory*, *The Colditz Story*, *The Bridge On The River Kwai*.
- **Retrosexual values:** Courage, strength and the strange ability to positively thrive in a world bereft of women.

The Gangster Movie

They might bully, torture and savagely murder their victims, but at least they live their lives by a moral code. With their *omerta* and their family values, they're Men of Honour, and how we love them for it. And, over and above wielding an indiscriminate machine-gun, they get to wear sharp suits and eat pasta. Cool.

- **Top selection:** *The Godfather*, *Goodfellas*, *Scarface*.
- **Retrosexual values:** They have great-looking women who never question their men's motives and blood-stained boots and are just happy to have the maître d' fawning over them in the restaurant.

Science Fiction

Men are fascinated by the technological promises and moral dilemmas of the future. Will time travel really be possible? Could it ever be right to erase someone's identity? Will they invent a pie that can be microwaved and not go soggy? And they have some brilliant weapons.

- **Top selection:** *The Terminator, Blade Runner, Mad Max 2.*
- **Retrosexual values:** The futuristic robot is a retrosexual dream – technologically sophisticated, devoid of emotion and acting purely on logic.

Schlock Horror

A genuine scarer (as opposed to the 'teen scream' genre) will leave you unsettled, jumping out of your skin at the faintest sound and having nightmares for weeks. But if you can face demons, pure evil and malicious spirits and still manage a smile and a 'That was fun' at the end, you'll come out of it looking more of a man than ever.

- **Top selection:** *The Evil Dead, The Exorcist, Nightmare on Elm Street.*
- **Retrosexual values:** The toughest test a man can face is not to be scared. Keep control of your bodily functions and you can claim some sort of victory.

Martial Arts

It takes inner resolution, complete control of your physical capabilities and intense concentration, but sit through a mind-numbing two and a half hours of pseudo-mystical cod-philosophy, ridiculous choreographed fights and incomprehensible dialogue, and you've cleared one of the great Retrosexual hurdles.

- **Top selection:** *Enter The Dragon, Crouching Tiger, Farting Dragon, Rumble In The Bronx, The Killing Machine.*
- **Retrosexual values:** You see that gang of 14-year-olds smashing up the bus stop? Wouldn't you love to leave every one of them on the deck gasping for breath instead of walking past with your head down, hoping they don't notice you?

The Sports Film

Sports movies notoriously lack authenticity and often just look like a load of pansy actors kicking balls like girls. The great ones, however, capture that locker-room tension so definitively you can almost smell the inflammable mix of body odour, testosterone, Deep Heat and star player out for retribution.

- **Top selection:** *Any Given Sunday, Raging Bull, Slap Shot.*
- **Retrosexual values:** The stuff of sport speaks for philosophy, love, life and death. What more could you want?

MEN INTO MEDICAL CARE WON'T GO

It's easier to get a man to go to the opera than to get him to a doctor. There have been numerous studies and campaigns, analyzing and cajoling reluctant men with nothing apparently wrong with them to see already overworked GPs, but nothing ever seems to change. And nothing ever will, as long as the official line continues to assert that men don't go to the doctor because of fear, denial and embarrassment when the real reasons are logical and perfectly acceptable.

A retrosexual knows there's usually little a doctor can do for him. Any pain he suffers – from a head wound to a bone emerging from the knee – can be reduced to an ache, a sprain or 'a little tightness that will disappear in the morning'. These can be easily treated by aspirin, alcohol, ignoring it and hoping the remarkable recuperative properties of the human body will do their stuff. Only when it turns green, falls off or stops him driving will he consider medical attention.

Even then, he has considerable reluctance to let a bloke tell him to drop his trousers, just because he has a beard and some impressive gadgets. Once they start poking around down there who knows what they'll find? Better to wait until you have at least three ailments requiring urgent attention. When you can barely walk, pissing is agony and your vision is constantly the same as if you'd downed a couple of bottles of vodka, no one can accuse you of taking it lightly.

Only then can the nightmare begin...

The Pre-Surgery Procedure

Most men will fail to clear the first hurdle: speaking to the receptionist. This is invariably a woman, whose first priority is to persuade you that you don't need to see a doctor. For someone not that bothered in the first place, it's a no-brainer. 'There are no appointments available for the next ten days,' she'll tell you, in which time you'll either have recovered or cut it off yourself with that Black and Decker you've been itching to use.

The Waiting Room

Waiting rooms are deliberately designed to scare men off. Firstly, they're full of sick people; secondly, nearly all of them are old women or young children, both of which are likely to drive a man not at his peak straight to the pub; and, finally, you have to wait. If you're lucky, you'll get to see a doctor within the hour – valuable time in which to assess whether it's that important anyway.

The Doctor Will See You Now

From the moment you step into the doctor's office, you know exactly what'll happen. To begin with, he/she will ask you how much you drink, you'll admit to about half the units you actually consume and, in his head, he'll multiply your answer by three. You'll then tell him exactly what's wrong with you according to your internet research and he'll get in a huff, ask about your prostate, threaten you with an anal probe and tell you to come back in two weeks if the symptoms haven't disappeared. So he's annoyed you by telling you that you drink too much, you've pissed him off and no one's any the wiser about what's wrong. Well worth it.

Retrosexual Ailments

Despite an unwillingness to seek medical help, retrosexual man is human and is prone to some of the most painful illnesses. What women are learning to admire is the admirable way in which he handles these situations. He's a picture of stoicism, usually lying on the sofa, watching daytime television, groaning 'I'm really very ill' in a desperate voice and re-reading the paracetamol package to see when he can take his next dose.

There are very few illnesses so debilitating that they can stop a man watching sport or going to the pub, but he is susceptible to the following:

Man Cold

The 'man cold' is a layman's term for a near-fatal illness often mistakenly associated with the kind of soft colds that afflict women. The resultant headache, runny nose and general feeling of queasiness can leave a man helpless. He is usually forced to rely on a nearby female to administer biscuits, Lemsip and whisky; and find him a TV channel which shows children's cartoons.

Hangovers

A bad hangover can leave a man reeling, with a head feeling as if someone's battering at it with a pneumatic drill, a tongue like a small furry creature and an unsteady mix of nausea and delirium. He is usually, understandably, frustrated, as there's very little he can do about it apart from pick up on some of his girlfriend's bad habits, keep repeating 'I didn't drink that much, it must be something I ate' and seek a suitably greasy cafe to administer the only possible cure of Red Bull and a bacon sandwich.

Football Injury

There was a time when a man limping or struggling around on crutches would be given due respect. It was assumed he'd received his injuries in the service of his country and had been a victim of a devious foreign sniper or, more probably, American friendly fire. These days, thankfully, our victims of war are fewer and such partially mobile men are looked down on as wastrels and soft cases – unless they're able to claim a football injury. If they can prove they received the blow in a proper match (not some kick-around with the nephews) and the affliction is a known injury as suffered by proper players – groin, calf, hamstring, metatarsal – only then can they hobble around with the consent and admiration of the population.

Festivalitis

The Cheltenham Festival comprises nearly a week of the best horse jump racing in the world; it has a fabulous, electrifying atmosphere despite most of the blokes there having reported to their bosses that they're at death's door. Throwing a sickie is an art. Many novices just go for the simple cold or a bad case of food poisoning, but these often arouse instant suspicion among employers. A little more imagination can earn you credibility and more than just a couple of days off (most companies allow the whole seven days without a doctor's note). Among the best are claiming a highly contagious skin disease, which can clear up in a few days with antibiotics and leave no visible marks, or the marvellous labyrinthitis, where you'll need to explain that it's an inner ear infection which affects your balance, meaning you have to lie down all day.

There are, however, a few basic rules to claiming a sickie:

- Pave the way the day before, occasionally complaining of pains or lethargy.
- Persuade your girlfriend or mum to ring in for you – but not your best mate.
- Try to ring in before your manager arrives at work and leave a message on the answerphone.
- Sound a little pathetic, but not too ill – unless your acting is up to it.
- Remember you only have four grandparents whose funerals you can attend.
- Try not to be seen out, avoid local pubs and local TV reporters doing vox pops.
- Ensure you carry on the act on your return – don't turn up with a fried egg sandwich, you are still 'ill' and could be prone to a relapse at any time.

PERSONAL GROOMING

'Personal grooming' was a phrase which came along in the 1980s. Until then, 'grooming' was something only associated with horses. For years men had been quite happy with the terms 'washing' and 'brushing their hair'. It had got them through world wars, depressions and even the Great Brylcreem Drought of 1951. This new phrase – neatly suggesting that men, like their equine friends, needed a good seeing-to with a stiff brush – had the convenience of tying up all the things guys were supposed to do to make themselves presentable new men. These would include hair styling, nasal and ear hair trimming, and manicures, and would eventually incorporate facial treatments and bodily hair removal.

The retrosexual naturally gives short shrift to these matters, but these are modern times and appearances are valued more highly than ever. The dilemma for a 24-carat bloke on the sniff is that he needs to show how little he values 'personal grooming' without coming across as if he's spent the week at the local doss-house.

The Retrosexual In The Bathroom

One of the great advantages of having a retrosexual as a boyfriend is that he won't take up valuable time in the bathroom. He's not going to spend hours preening in front of the mirror, wallowing in a tealight-surrounded bath or covering himself in ointments. To put it bluntly – as we've already learned – he's purely a shit, shave and shower man.

- A retrosexual does not pluck or shave any part of his body below the neck.
- The only time a retrosexual gets into a bath with bubbles is if invited by a woman.
- The retrosexual's only use for a bidet is to wash his feet.
- A retrosexual will have one bottle of aftershave – bought for him by an auntie seven years ago.
- A retrosexual has no moisturizer, massage oils or skin balm – but has a sachet (unopened) of something he has never heard of which dropped out of a magazine.

The Haircut

Take a look in the mirror and assess the kind of hair you have been blessed with. Is your hair curly or straight? Is it wavy, bushy or easily manageable? Do you have an abundance of hair or are you starting to thin or even go bald? Fortunately for you, it doesn't matter in the slightest. And stop looking in the mirror now.

Although cutting your own hair is an attractive proposition, it's not really advisable, as you run the risk of being taken into care or mistaken for a singer in an indie band. Should you opt for a hairdresser or a barber? What do you think? Here are some hints.

- The only place a retrosexual makes appointments is at the car mechanics or the STD clinic.
- After giving the barber brief but precise instructions, you remain silent – no discussions about holidays, Princess Diana conspiracies or hair thinning treatments.
- No, you do not want a coffee, a hair-wash, a blow-dry or anything that will delay your exit by more than a second.
- No, you do not want anything on it – particularly some gel that makes you smell like the ground floor at Selfridge's.

The hair is one of a very limited number of opportunities men have to express their individuality. Dyeing your hair an outlandish colour can demand attention, building an impressive tower of hair can gain curious looks or you could just GET SOME CHARACTER and not feel the need to look like a complete prat. However, being a retrosexual doesn't necessary mean you have to get a short back and sides. A quick look at some common hairstyles can give us some alternative ideas.

- **Scalp:** do you really want to be shaving your head every two days, just so no one knows you've got a virtually bald pate anyway? Popular with Nazis, footballers, students and in Old Compton Street bars. Avoid.
- **Short hair:** ideal for the man who doesn't want to try too hard – a number two all over in the summer, letting the top grow out for some added heat in winter. It doesn't need combing and gives you the appearance of someone who can handle themselves in a fight, but can makes the round-faced chap's head look like a football or can frizz up to resemble an oversize tennis ball.
- **Medium-length hair:** usually worn by short hair-wearers who delay their trip to the barber's. However, a Sean Penn-style, messed-up medium-length cut can attract the women with that just-got-out-of-bed kind of look. Good for those with thinning hair, but can take a while to dry. Remember the retrosexual wouldn't be seen dead with a hairdryer.
- **Long hair:** if you can be bothered and really want to do this, go ahead; it's the 21st century now and blokes with long hair can get the girls. But there are some rules: no ponytails (Status Quo ruined everyone's fun), no layering (ahhh! The 1980s!) and, as soon as it touches the shoulders, you get it snipped.

- **The bowl cut:** just because it looked good on you when you were nine doesn't mean it's still appropriate. The only person you'll remind people of is Damien from *The Omen*, and that isn't a good look.
- **The mullet:** are you German? No? Then leave it alone.
- **The comb-over:** a very useful hairstyle for balding men, allowing them to cover up their hairless patches effectively. Who are you kidding? Your mum might be nice about it, but everyone else thinks you're a knobend.
- **Dreadlocks:** stylish, with attitude and 100 per cent male, providing you are black, come from the Caribbean and are in a reggae band. Otherwise, you're a public-school vegan drop-out, still living off daddy's money, who might as well wear a big badge saying, 'I like cannabis, me.'
- **The Lloyd Webber (also known as the Trump):** the style of hair that just slops down over your head in an uncontrollable fashion can say, 'I realize I look completely stupid, but I just don't give a toss.' Perfect for millionaires who can get any girl they want anyway.

Manicures

The only manicure men used to get was when they got a little too close to the belt sander. Now we read that men are regularly getting their nails trimmed and filed and their cuticles pushed back. Of course they are. On building sites across the country they're remarking, 'Give me a hand with this girder, Mac. Blimey! Haven't you got lovely smooth fingernails?' Don't be fooled by the name. There's no room for a 'man' in a manicure.

Nasal and Ear Hair

'Embarrassed about your nasal hair?' scream the trimmer ads. 'No,' we snap back in reply. The same way we're not embarrassed about holes in our socks, farting in bed, wearing the same underpants on consecutive days and drinking milk from the carton, because we're men and have better things to do with our time than pick infinitesimally small hairs from places where we might well need them, like, for example, studying the Scottish Third Division league table.

Facial Hair

What could be more manly than facial hair? A symbol of virility, maturity, social standing, non-conformity and counter-cultural identity, a beard or moustache will surely set you apart from the nonces, dandies and puffed-up fops of today. Or will it? The world of facial hair is a minefield; tread carefully...

The Chin Curtain: the beard that follows the jaw-line but not on to the face is one favoured by Abraham Lincoln, the Amish community and socially-challenged people who work in IT – none of whom you need to be associated with.

The Goatee: Buffalo Bill, Lenin, Freud, Colonel Sanders, Bruce Willis, even the devil has worn one; you think they're pretty cool, eh? Oh, you work in the media, are an Apple obsessive and have enough time between reading Manga comics to constantly trim the thing?

The Goatee, Moustache and Shaved Head Combination: you look like a bloke who's gone mad in prison and is being forced to spend the rest of his 672-year sentence in solitary – and you think girls are going to like this? We're trying to look like a real man here, not as if we'd like to eat one.

The Handlebar Moustache: a bold move. You're the last remaining member of the Tufnell Park Hell's Angels chapter or are trying some kind of retro gay look – either way, best of luck.

The Fu Manchu: your exotic rebel chic might sit well in the Hoxton bar, but then people discover you work in a bank...

THE SPORTING RETROSEXUAL

Sport is at the heart of the man. It gives him something to do on Saturday afternoons, Sunday afternoons, Monday evenings and often in the week as well. It gives him something to talk about and a reason to buy a newspaper. It is where he feels most comfortable, most intense and most able to communicate with his fellow men – and it is his world, one which a woman will never understand.

It is the enigma of this relationship which strikes at the souls of women. The bond man has with sport (OK, let's come clean and call it football) is something she can never have: the highs and lows, the inability to disengage, the emotional release. How frustrating and tantalizing it must be to see he has all these qualities, but is unable to apply them to his soulmate.

Loyalty

A man can stand at the altar and agree to stick by his bride 'for richer, for poorer, 'til death do us part', but deep down he knows there's always a way out: a quickie divorce, a moonlit flit or a pile of clothes and a note left on the beach. But with his team, there can never be an escape. The board can sell out to genocidal dictators, set ticket prices that are the equivalent of a small house or knock the ground down and build an anodyne 'Euro stadium' 12 miles out of town, but so long as they play in your team's name and the kit bears a fleeting resemblance to the one you bought when you were nine years old, you're stuck with them.

Things A Man Is Only Able To Do At A Football Match

- Chant.
- Pray.
- Indulge in superstitions such as wearing his underpants inside-out.
- Scream with pain.
- Talk to a stranger.
- Sit in serene contemplation.

Loving The Hurt

No real man supports a team for its success. Snatching defeat from the jaws of victory, relegation, bankruptcy (see where we're going with this one, Leeds United fans?) are all collected as scars of life. These are the real medals of the football supporter. The more abject their performance, the more your team are testing your faith, and the more Arsenal and Manchester United flaunt their pretty-foreign-boy football, the better you feel for clinging to your home-grown hoofers and cloggers.

Language

This isn't meant to exclude women – and the new football-loving men (aka the Prawn Sandwich Brigade). It's great that they're interested in the game and they often have a better understanding of tactics and appreciation of skill than the retrosexual, but, like a foreigner fluent in a second language, they'll never fully understand the nuances and subtle changes of tone used by a native. They might know their 4–3–3 from a 4–4–2, but they'll never feel the true meaning of 'What's that c**t doing out on the wing?' They can applaud a fine goal against the run of play, but when a retrosexual shouts, 'Fuck me, fucking fuck me, he's fucking done it!' there's a whole history of emotion and meaning hidden behind the vocabulary.

Emotional Distress

Tune in to any post-match football phone-in and you'll hear the kind of despair, anguish and hopelessness that a Samaritan would wait a lifetime for: men staring into the abyss, all because their team could only manage a draw at Oldham. Women, of course, feel like this at least 12 times a day – they've missed the bus, a fingernail breaks, someone forgets to buy milk – but these are men who switch off their mother's life-support with not a tear, who seem unable to hug their children, choking over a game which happened 16 years ago.

Other Sports

No other sport can capture the heart of the retrosexual quite like football, but it should be the inalienable right of any man to watch any sport on television whenever he chooses – even if it coincides with the final of *X-Factor* or the news on a day when the Pope, the Queen and Chris Martin have been assassinated. Most men can take anything Eurosport 3 throws at them – powerboat-racing, shove-ha'penny, non-beach volleyball, endless marathons, even tennis – but somehow they still can't quite get the point of synchronized swimming.

Things A Retrosexual Doesn't Do At Football

- Sit in hospitality boxes and miss the start of the second half because he's finishing his *tarte au citron*.
- Go along to the game 'because there should be a good atmosphere'.
- Leave before the final whistle.
- Applaud the opposition.
- Shout anything which doesn't include an expletive.
- Get there an hour early to wander around the club megastore.
- Eat anything, apart from a hot dog that might well be made with real dog.

Participation

Some men will go so far as to participate in a sport, even after they've left school. The retrosexual may choose to play football, rugby or cricket at any level, but whether he is playing park-standard or semi-professional, he is completely committed – to his club, to his team and to the team-building social events (ie after-match drinking). Weddings, funerals, anniversaries and births of offspring all come a poor second to the match. In fact, the only things which can stop him turning out in the team's colours are a bad hangover, heavy rain and the promise of 'special' sex – and even then he'll probably make it to the after-match drinks.

The Sporting Equivalent Of Castration

There are, however, certain sports which should be given a wide berth. Far from being seen as a testosterone-pumping, sweat-dripping, exotic and erotic being from another planet, you'll look like a sad misfit who's too scared to try a proper sport.

- **Mixed softball:** for all you bowl her easy, underarm balls, demonstrate how to hold the bat and 'accidentally' miss the plate, she'll still end up snogging the smug twat from your rival advertising agency.
- **Badminton:** 'Shall we not bother scoring?' No, why bother even hitting the shuttlecock over the net? In fact, just get changed and go straight to the bar, it'll save the pretence.
- **Tennis:** it's Wimbledon week, you've got your sparkling whites, your brand-new expensive racket and you've cleared the kids on bicycles off the court. Now you've got to work out just how it's possible to get the ball over the net, but not over the fence and into the boating lake.
- **American football:** yes, of course you need a helmet and padding just in case a big boy falls on top of you.
- **Choi Kwang Do:** a non-contact martial art? Round our way we call that dancing.

YOU ARE WHAT YOU DRIVE

The truth is simple: a retrosexual needs a car like a dog needs a collar. Without it you are a stray – an intellectual, a student, a chav or an environmentalist – and most birds will give you a wide berth. According to a government survey, 66 per cent of women want their man to own or have access to a car. They might not like the way you drive or the mess on the back seat or the abuse you give to old men in hats, but somewhere deep within them they are equating horsepower with sexual attraction and, if you haven't got wheels, it's you who's travelling unleaded.

Although he's reticent in demonstrating warmth in his relationships, a retrosexual's relationship with his car is special. He's the only one who's permitted to wash it, he's protective of it – always aware of the threat, or potential threat, of someone scratching or scraping it – and is happy to display signs of affection such as patting the steering wheel, car roof or dashboard, and glancing back at it as if to say goodbye.

This relationship is also clear when he's in the driving seat. Confident in his vehicle, he always drives with one hand on the steering wheel, leaving the other free to adjust the music, caress the gear-stick in anticipation or make abusive gestures to cyclists. The Retrosexual isn't one to fall easily into a road rage, but he'll maintain eye contact with all other drivers and never misses an opportunity to pass comment on anyone driving too fast, slowly, recklessly, carefully, aggressively, timidly... well, anyone, really.

A seemingly encyclopaedic knowledge of the Highway Code enables him to accurately criticize every other driver's road sense ('Come on; I have right of way when I'm driving round a corner on a hill if there's an ice-cream van that's been parked for more than 30 seconds. You should know that, Mr Toilet Paper Salesman, with your "So many pedestrians, so little time" bumper sticker'), but, over and above this, the retrosexual has his own driving code.

- Always drive at a speed that is five per cent over the limit.
- Always keep a maximum distance of three feet between you and the car in front.
- Use your common sense when deciding to let someone in at a junction. Is she good-looking? If not, don't bother.
- Your lane is always the slowest. It's your duty to get into the next one.
- If you stop at a crossing, make sure pedestrians know how fortunate they are by waving them across.
- When passing a cyclist, drive as close to them as possible and stare at them as if they've just landed from another planet.
- Avoid the left-hand lane of the motorway. It's for lorries, caravans and people who've only just passed their driving test.

- Indicating for a left turn is pointless. They'll find out soon enough.
- The horn should only be used to wake up someone in front of you who's asleep at the lights (short parp), to discover if a woman has a decent face as well as a good body (two short parps) or to challenge a fellow-road user to a pointless shouting match and possible fisticuffs (a long parp followed by 30 seconds of invective).

What Your Car Says About You

As much as she might tut and sigh at your style of driving, she'll know she's in the safe-ish care of a real man. She'll realize there's no chance of you suddenly stopping at a zebra crossing as she's putting on her make-up or refusing to give her a lift to the hairdresser's because it'll cause the ice caps to melt. But does it matter what you drive? Will it affect your retrosexual status and pulling ability? You bet.

In the 1970s, when men drove cars without fear of being accused of gas-guzzling, giving asthma to our children and 'showing off like a 17-year-old who's just passed his test' (OK, maybe that one was just me), they drove Capris and Granadas, Avengers and Rovers. Their cars had panache and oomph and were within the pockets of working men. Women were grateful just to get a lift and as long as you had wheels, you were in.

Then came the 1980s, when it seemed women were only interested in anyone who drove a Porsche 911 or a Ferrari Testarossa (which basically came down to city boys with red braces), and the 1990s, when they realized they could afford their own sports cars and could ditch the wanker in the driving seat.

Today, as in the other walks of life we've looked at, a woman is looking for a man to be behind the wheel of a real man's car. It doesn't have to be sporty or sleek, a convertible or a Humvee power monster, but it does have to say you're a testosterone-fuelled, red-blooded man.

Cars A Retrosexual Can Happily Drive

Coupes and roadsters. Want to see how a man can truly love his car far more than any woman? Give a bloke a Mazda RX8 or an Audi TT, let him cruise with the windows down and the stereo up and then tell me the retrosexual has no soul.

Estates and MPVs. The geezer with a practical motor such as a Volvo V70, Vauxhall Zafira, Renault Scenic or Toyota Verso isn't trying to make a statement. It's just a car, right? But somehow, it seems at ease with him and his mentality.

Convenience cars. He's sat there in his Mondeo Ghia, Honda Accord or Peugeot 406 wishing he had something a bit tastier, but at least it's reliable and his bird never has to know that he doesn't understand a thing the mechanic's talking about.

Cars A Retrosexual Wouldn't Be Seen Dead In

BMWs. No need to make yourself even more unpopular. Just leave them to the drug-dealers and people with anger management problems.

Hot hatches. Stylish, reliable and they can pack a punch – so why is there always a suspicion that your wife made you buy it?

The New Mini. Doesn't lack style or oomph, but you'll get people asking, 'Is that two-bedroom flat on Park Street still on the market?'

Automatics. What's wrong with using a clutch? Scared of making that clunking noise or just plain lazy? There's something about masterly use of the gear-stick that can drive a woman wild. Look at James Hunt.

Dinky toys. OK, blokes who go for big motors have all got little dicks, so what's someone who drives a Twingo or a Ka lacking in – apart from a little more power than a lawnmower on wheels?

White van. Now you're not taking this seriously...

Your Pulling Machine

So you've got the right kind of driving technique and a real retrosexual vehicle, but you're still finding girls would rather get the bus. Just maybe you've chosen the wrong colour car. A survey commissioned by insurance company Churchill found that women viewed the colour of a car as much more important than its shape or size. More than 50 per cent said they'd try to have a closer look at a driver, and 10 per cent admitted having a date with a man, because the colour of his car created a good impression.

If you've got a tasteful new mannish pistachio or ever-cleaned white machine, therefore, get it down the garage for a paint job. Silver, black and red, in that order, are the colours which get the ladies' engines running. Just as well, then, that almost every bloke in the country has a silver, black or red motor.

6. THE MATURE RETROSEXUAL

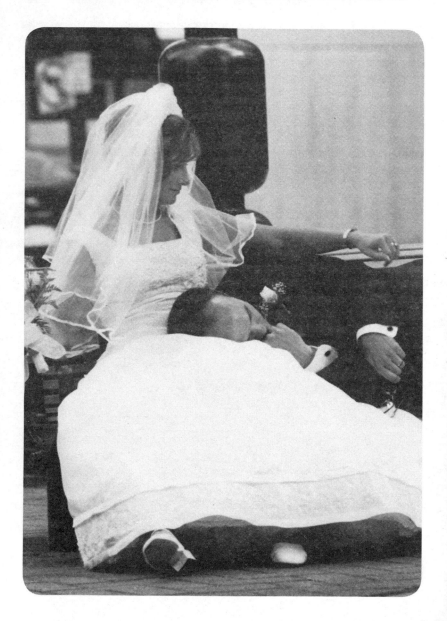

The following pages deal with the problem of maintaining your life as a retrosexual as the years progress. It may no longer be an attempt to pull the birds (although, amazingly, many's the young girl who sees something in the older man), but a necessity in order to keep the respect of the woman now in your life.

Whether you're 23 or 43, sooner or later the time's going to come when you see those thrilling days of throwing up outside the kebab shop at 2am, waking up with someone who looks like your Aunt Gladys or travelling 450 miles to see your team scrape a 0–0 draw in a god-forsaken Yorkshire dump drifting away. This is the growing up thing they always warned you about.

But it needn't be all bad. If you can get the right work–leisure balance (somewhere around 10 percent–90 percent), find yourself a decent woman and maintain your dignity as a man, you may well yet find yourself with another 40 or 50 years of almost tolerable life.

ENGAGEMENT

There's only so much a man can take. Once one of her friends has got engaged, your girlfriend will start to turn up the pressure and it won't stop until you're emerging from Argos with the ring. Modern women have techniques of which the Spanish Inquisition would be proud. They'll tell your friends of your imminent union, start collecting useful nick-nacks for the new house and open discussions on possible honeymoon destinations – and that's after you've been seeing her for two months.

You can try putting it off with 'I'm just not ready' or 'Shouldn't we save up a little?' or even 'I'm thinking of joining the Moonies' or 'I've a life-threatening illness and could die any time in the next couple of months' – but eventually they'll wear you down. The problem then is that doing nothing is no longer an option. Just agreeing that an engagement would be a good thing isn't enough; they want you on your knees...

THE PROPOSAL

Christ! It's the 21st century! You might be forgiven for thinking we'd moved on from that kind of Jane Austen scenario by now, but no. It seems every woman still dreams that in some kind of Faustian transformation you're going to haul your arse off the sofa and suddenly come over all romantic. In a recent poll, women ranked the day their boyfriends proposed as the most eagerly anticipated event of their lives, even before their wedding day, and 85 percent stated that they were 'disappointed' in the way they were proposed to (never mind, though: 81 percent said they'd never reveal that much to their boyfriends).

In your mind, of course, humiliating yourself by going down on one knee like a complete berk is the last thing you're planning to do. This also applies to other romantic options such as returning to the place where you first met or writing 'Will you marry me?' in condensation on the bedroom window. As a retrosexual, your task is to see how casual you can play it, short of getting your mate to ask for you.

Times You Might Be Tempted To Propose But Really Shouldn't

- Right after she tells you she's pregnant.
- At McDonald's ('Hey, babe, what's that under your slice of gherkin?')
- In the middle of a row ('There's your fucking ring: happy now?')
- Over the tannoy at the football (think how you'll look if she says no).
- When you're drunk and not in full command of your senses.

Getting the tone right for the big moment is essential. Try to practice popping the question when you're alone in the house. You're usually only going to get one go at this, so you've got to get it right. A great retrosexual will hit the perfect note, expressing it in a way that simultaneously could mean:

- I really, really love you and want us to spend the rest of our lives together.
- I can take it or leave it, really, I'm just trying to be nice here.
  [And, in case she turns you down]
- Only joking, it was just a wind-up, honest.

Too sentimental and romantic and you're setting yourself standards for life that you can never live up to, but if you say it as if you really don't care, you'll be reminded of it for the rest of your days. There are numerous ways in which you can approach the subject, but here are a few you may wish to consider:

- In a text message ('I'll be home L8r, can u get the KFC in and will u mrry me?')
- In the TV ad break ('Put the kettle on, love, oh, and...')
- During the match ('I wondered what you thought of... oh, come on! That must have been offside!')
- The indirect approach ('So, when are we going to go and get the ring?')
- The rational approach ('I've been checking out the tax allowances and...')

THE RING

Be on your guard. Just as men are born instinctively knowing the names of the 1966 World Cup-winning team, so all women seem to know the mantra about the fiancé waving goodbye to at least a month's salary for an engagement ring. She'll soon be going on about the 'Four Cs' of diamonds – cut, colour, clarity and carat.

At this point you need to assess your situation. You've just made the biggest concession to a woman a man can ever make. You're setting yourself up for a lifetime of gratuitous expenditure and debt. You're going to have to buy another ring in nine months' time for the wedding. Do you really want to be one of the 75 per cent of men who buy their 'special lady' a diamond engagement ring?

Now, if you want to avoid her using other 'c' words, such as cheapskate, callous and c*nt, it's time to mobilize 'Four Cs' of your own...

- Christmas cracker ring: you can argue that you pulled it in a shared moment, that it represents two halves of the same thing and it has a unique romantic quality.
- Conscience: does she realize the planet's key diamond mines are found in areas such as Sierra Leone, Rwanda and Liberia, and help inflame some of the world's bitterest conflicts?
- Courtesy: OK, she might find your grandmother's ring unfashionable, grotesque and hideous, but she'd be performing the utmost courtesy in agreeing to be part of the family.
- Cubic zirconia: almost indistinguishable from a diamond (to those who don't know what a diamond looks like), it is freely available from most home shopping channels.

THE STAG PARTY

However long the gap between your engagement and your wedding, it'll be too long. It's a time of deliberation and debate: the present list, the guest list, the honeymoon destination and all the time you're wondering how to tell her you want to call the whole thing off. While your lovely bride-to-be frets over whether the bridesmaids' dresses clash with the church curtains, whether her gran might choke on the salmon starter and where on earth to seat your obnoxious mate Kevin whom she hates with a vengeance (and whom you haven't actually told her is going to be your best man), you have only one thing on your mind: the stag party.

Once it was enough to have a night out with your mates before the big day. True enough, you'd get completely pissed, sometimes be stripped bollock-naked and possibly be chained to a lamp-post in the high street. Oh, such innocent times! The next day you'd arrive at the church with a punishing hangover, unable to remember a thing about the night and wondering why her aunt was grinning at you like that.

Now, the stag do is bigger than the wedding. If it's not a weekend indulging in the tacky delights of Newquay or Blackpool, it's a trip to Prague or Budapest to visit authentic beer cellars full of pissed-up Brits from Liverpool, Newcastle and Brum. No self-respecting geezer will consider they've had a good time if they haven't got on the wrong plane and landed up in Aberdeen, been thrown into a police cell for two days until they sobered up and contracted a rare sexually-transmitted disease only previously known to goats. And, now the whole of Eastern Europe has been opened up, it's not unlikely that from Warsaw to Lithuania you might find yourself starkers, mud-wrestling with two blonde beauties and, in exactly the same spot your grandfather was trying to tunnel out of when incarcerated during World War Two.

The difference between the stag parties of yore and today is that whereas they used to be seen as the final kick of a dying man before the shackles of domesticity were fastened, now they're a defiant gesture declaring, 'This is my life and woe betide the woman who tries to stop me.' The stakes in outrageous behaviour are continually being raised, but a selection of activities from the following menu should provide enough self-respect to see you through the first few years of marriage:

- Write off your go-kart as you desperately try to stop your best man from winning.
- Get thrown off the plane for making lewd suggestions to the stewardess.
- Indulge in perverse sexual acts with a group of Danish sailors.
- Get arrested for exposing yourself in front of a national monument.

- Spend time in a foreign jail for an obscure crime such as farting on public transport between 3.30 and 5pm on a Wednesday.
- Fall in love with an East European prostitute and pay for her air ticket to London.
- Have to rely on the British Embassy to find your clothes, passport, hotel and a reason for living.
- Undergo a personality change for six months after imbibing mind-addling absinthe cocktails.
- Pick a fight with a crack SAS platoon on R&R from Afghanistan.

HOW NOT TO BE A GROOMZILLA

For years men have walked in fear of Bridezilla, the sweet-natured fiancée who is somehow transformed into a scenery-chewing monster, but in recent years, as the metrosexuals mature, we have witnessed the birth of Groomzilla. These men insist on attending wedding shows, spending every waking minute with wedding planners, throwing hissy-fits over the floral arrangements and sending caterers running for cover.

As much as brides traditionally whined that their man didn't seem at all interested in the colour of the tablecloths or whether little Sean would make a good pageboy, imagine how much worse they felt when the Groomzilla really did show an interest, began interfering and really taking over. That's why they welcome the retrosexual with open arms.

Still, it's important that you don't leave all the organization to your bride – and, no doubt, her mother. As a commitment to your future wife, you must be willing to ease her load and take on some of the burden, while still recognizing there are elements she will enjoy being in control of. If you can, adhere to the following recommended lines of demarcation:

Her
- Choose date and book venue.
- Choose the dress, bridesmaids' outfits and bridegroom's suit.
- Organize cars and transport.
- Hotel reservations.
- Invitations.
- Catering, including wedding cake.
- Table decorations.
- Place-settings.
- Select aisle and first dance music.
- Book honeymoon.

Him
- Sort DJ out.
- Choose wine.
- Make sure she hasn't hired a kilt for you.

If you find you don't have time to fulfil all these duties, just make sure you do the last. She'll pick up the other two, but it might be worth having a word in the DJ's ear about exactly how much R&B you're able to stand in one night.

THE BIG DAY

You're a retrosexual – a proud, self-reliant, independent thinker. You've gone ahead with the wedding even though you've had plenty of time to reconsider, so it's safe to assume that you can face this monumental day in your life with equanimity. But there's nobody and nothing that says you have to enjoy it.

So you've got the in-laws invading your house, you have to wear a suit for the first time since your court case, you couldn't be bothered writing a speech, your best man's lost the ring, the two families are squaring up for a fight, you're caught flirting with the maid of honour and your wife's in floods of tears over something you can't even remember saying. Just savour a few pints before the vows and a glass or two of tequila for Dutch courage before your speech, and it'll all pass in a blur – the happiest day of your life!

DAZED AND CONFUSED: MARRIAGE

Your life's no different, you tell yourself, just because you signed a bit of paper. You've already told her how you'll still be going to the football, going out on Friday nights with your mates and that you don't do supermarkets. And you really think you're going to be able to carry on for ever in denial, as if the marriage never happened. Think again, Buster. The retrosexual's biggest battle has just begun and, if you get out of this in one piece, you're a better man than most.

Household Chores

This will come as a complete revelation. There's a whole world of cleaning, polishing and washing you never thought possible. You'll find the cushions actually come off the sofa to reveal enough old bits to make a whole 12-inch pizza, 43 biros and coinage that was taken out of circulation in 1967. You'll discover that the bath didn't come with that dark ring half-way up it and the self-cleaning oven wasn't up to dealing with the burnt-on takeaway curry you spilled three years ago. The wife'll expect you do to your fair share of chores and your only way out of it is to do them really badly so she gives up on you, and to make sure she realizes you're taking responsibility for man's work such as mowing the lawn, cleaning the car and checking the loft insulation.

Socializing

Your nights of pub, darts and kebab are now under direct threat as pressure comes to go out with other married couples. Your single friends, some of whom she even slept with, will now be viewed as bad influences, freaks and perverts. Then, while your pissed-up mates at the club are chatting up a group of 17-year-old girls, you're being forced to listen to the new James Blunt album while eating 'something from Jamie's latest' and talking about house prices all night. But there's worse to come. When you do finally manage to arrange a lager-fuelled night out, she wants to come with you – thus breaking every rule in the retrosexual book.

Sex

Every couple's sex life is going to be different, some going at it hammer and tongs every day, others settling into a 'birthdays, bank holidays and blue moons' rota. But one thing's for sure – your domesticity will ensure it's the same again. Instead of having, 'Oh, God! Give it to me, now! Now! Now!' gasped at you in the throes of ecstasy, you'll hear, 'Oh, God! We forgot to put the recycling out!' And, sensational as she might look in her Wonder Woman outfit, you'll never quite be able to forget that this is the woman who caught you having one off the wrist while watching *Richard and Judy*.

Diet

It won't be long before strange objects begin appearing in the kitchen. Say hello to the vegetable. Your weekly meals will now be planned with such military precision that she's able to tell you what your evening meal will be on any given day in the next five years – and the odds are against there being any meat involved. Your stomach will grind for the want of bacon grease and your digestion system will be crippled through having to eat salad which hasn't even been sitting out for three days. Eventually the day will come when you, too, can't face the thought of leftover takeaway curry for breakfast.

For Ever Is A Long, Long Time

It's that nagging doubt that, however good it feels right now, in the long game you're on to a loser, as three out of five marriages fail in the first five years. You'll feel the grinding pressure of 'for ever' every time a girl catches your eye and smiles, every time her mother comes to stay 'just for a few days' and every time you wake her up at 3am having lost your keys.

Let's Make A Baby

There are enough tell-tale signs: her pregnant friends, her disappearing career ambitions, her contraceptive pills being flushed down the toilet and the fact that all of a sudden she's interested in having sex more than once a fortnight. She's decided the clock's ticking, and won't be happy until she's right up the duff. But, when it happens, it'll still come as a bolt from the blue. You'll walk around stupidly proud that everyone will know you're still shooting with live ammunition, but unaware that it could be your route back to Retrosexuality...

Raising a Retrosexual

Becoming a father is just about the proudest moment in any man's life, but for the retrosexual it offers something else – a way out of the matrimonial straitjacket. There are many lessons a man learns when he and his wife bring home their new baby: the realization of how precious life itself can be, the envy of a life devoted solely to sleeping and feeding, and the discovery that, as a parent, he's totally redundant. There's absolutely nothing a newborn baby wants from a great hairy oaf of a father when he has the attention of his soft, milk-providing, cuddling mother.

And yet, there he is, with paternity leave – anything from two to six weeks on full pay to spend 'not getting in mine and the baby's way'. Now, he could spend the time in the garage meticulously building an amazingly intricate Victorian doll's house or putting together a tiny replica Formula One car. Or he could usefully spend the time rediscovering his inner bloke – in the pub, at the bookie's and at the match. After all, there's no pressure to spend cozy nights in front of the fire any more; she's asleep by 8.30pm, and it's not even as if he's required in the bed any more – after the second time he's drunkenly rolled over on to the baby, he's going to be exiled to the spare room anyway. Hey ho, it's just like being a single man again.

If your child turns out to be a boy – your wife should let you know if this is the case, sooner or later – you'll have the added, onerous responsibility of raising a retrosexual. It falls upon you to ensure the boy grows up to be a proper bloke and avoids the many pitfalls which could lead him into a life of facepacks, espadrilles and working for a post-production company in Soho. Firstly, you'll be his role model and as such your retrosexual credentials must be impeccable. Secondly, you must watch and help him through any of the problem phases in his formulative years.

Pre-School

In every playgroup there's always one slightly unruly, aggressive, destructive and shouty child. What a disappointment it is when you discover it's not yours. If you find he prefers quietly painting in the corner to bombing smaller kids on the bouncy castle, or likes nothing better than sitting down with a picture book rather than experimenting by banging a large stick against a window, it might be time for that father-to-son chat. Is he developing an unnatural interest in what clothes he wears? Does he like playing with the girls? Has he yet to develop a hearty belch on downing his juice? Have a word.

School

The years between 9 and 15 are fraught with difficulties. A child has to learn to deal with friendship, a developing body, bullying, disappointment and an unrequited love for the French assistant. It's often difficult to find the right time to explain why you insist he has your old poster of Bobby Moore up on his wall. As it's important you take an interest in and monitor his progress at school, some of the following guidelines from the yet-to-be-published National Retrosexual Curriculum may be of some help.

- By the age of 8: is effectively running contraband tuckshop of banned crisps, sweets and chocolate.
- By the age of 9: spends his break times throwing wet tennis balls at velocity towards other pupils' heads.
- By the age of 10: understands the rules of darts and pool, and can fill in for the pub team.
- By the age of 11: has mastered scrunching up his school tie to a minuscule knot that sits three or four inches below the collar.
- By the age of 12: has his first girlfriend for two weeks before dumping her for her best friend.
- By the age of 13: has dropped art, English literature and sociology and is taking woodwork, design technology and metalwork.

- By the age of 14: is forced (by you) to return to the pub the day after being violently sick with alcohol poisoning.
- By the age of 15: is escorted (by you) on a visit to a prostitute for his first sexual encounter.
- By the age of 16: is prepared to stand his round – especially when his old man's forgotten his wallet.
- By the age of 17 and four months: has three points on his driving licence.
- By the age of 18: has left full-time education and enrolled in the University of Life.

The Divorce

Q. How many men does it take to change a light bulb in a divorced man's house?
A: Yeah, like he gets the house!

It's perfectly possible for a retrosexual to have an enduring, contented, lifelong marriage: possible, but not very likely. 75 percent of divorces are instigated by women and the chances are that you're never even going to see it coming. OK, you don't have sex any more – well, not with her, although she never really seemed that keen anyway; you don't spend much time together – although you did spend three hours sitting next to her recently when your boy was in A&E; and she's become indifferent to your indifference – but it doesn't mean you don't love her.

Maybe you should have noticed when she started collecting your payslips or when she started leaving the paper open for you on the Bedsits For Rent page. Perhaps that marriage counsellor was right – you should have taken the second honeymoon instead of going to watch England play in Kazakhstan – but it's too late now. Once you've bothered opening those divorce papers (you've never been a good reader and the free pizza delivery leaflet did seem more interesting), hang on to that shirt on your back...

Post-Divorce

So you're back on your Jack, but hold back those tears. You've got your own flat and absolutely no responsibilities. If you've played the whole divorce thing right, you'll still be on speaking terms with your ex and stand a good chance of getting your washing done and a decent Sunday roast, and you're back in the field with the one thing you were missing as a young retrosexual, 10 or so years earlier – an ex-wife.

Women love the older retrosexual. They admire the way he's withstood the emotional warfare of separation (when really the only tears he shed came as he said goodbye to the dog) and the ease with which he adapts to his independent lifestyle. They sense a certain sadness behind the eyes (probably the early development of cataracts), and find his greying hair and pot belly strangely attractive.

For the man himself, this can still be a stressful time. After all, his young days have seemingly been wasted and the love he's nurtured and cared for has dried up and died. It's difficult to decide whether to call up his ex's best mate who always flirted with him or try for someone a little younger, whether to buy a BMW convertible or a Harley: and for how many consecutive nights he can eat takeaways wearing just his underpants.

Tell-tale Signs Your Divorce Isn't Going Well...

- Your wife's lawyer is seeking the death penalty.
- Your mother's name appears on your wife's witness list.
- You get the kids every other weekend, which coincides with your team's home games.
- Your part of the settlement consists solely of the mini-fridge and the *Tomb Raider* video game.
- The judge is considering your wife's request for custody of your immortal soul.
- You have to return your 'World's Greatest Lover' mug.
- You might only get to see your inner child every other Wednesday.
- Your wife's requested that you pay the alimony directly to her Swiss bank account.
- In her search for hidden assets, your wife's hired a proctologist.

THE RETROSEXUAL OAP

Just because when you nod off everyone thinks you've died or people ring up at 9pm saying, 'I hope I didn't wake you', there's still no need to give up your retrosexual values. Right until he breathes his last, the ageing bloke can still be a force to be reckoned with.

The great advantage is that now you're a senior citizen you can get away with so many of the things you've been castigated for in your younger days. Your clothes can smell, you don't have to bathe for weeks on end, you can sit at the bar with piss-stains down your trousers and still mouth obscenities to young women. You can get a disabled parking badge, a mobility vehicle, whistle through your nose when you speak and legitimately choose not to hear anything anyone says – and, at last, you get to wear elasticated trousers.

Best of all, thanks to Viagra (generic name Mycoxafailin) you can now keep on at it well into old age. If you're going to get to use it, you're going to have to go to the bingo, get on buses, be willing to sit through 500 pictures of their grandchildren and not make disparaging comments about Sir Cliff, but if you can bear the scent of all that lavender there are rich pickings out there, although it's best not to book dirty weekends away longer than a month in advance and try not to panic every time you wake up to find her unconscious.

Senior Citizens' Chat-Up Lines

- Do you believe in love at first sight or are your cataracts playing tricks on you?
- I've lost my London Underground map. Can I use the veins in your leg?
- I love your vest, corset, other vest, blouse, pullover, cardigan, scarf, coat, shawl and self-knitted woolly hat, but I think they'd look better on my bedroom floor.
- Is that smell from your colostomy bag or are you just pleased to see me?
- I see your glass is empty. Do you mind if I put my teeth in it?

THE BIG 'D'

In the end, we all meet the one thing we can't ignore, laugh off or punch in the face: death. But who wants to breathe their last surrounded by weeping relatives or dribbling in a care home while watching *Teletubbies*? The retrosexual must attempt to die in the same style he tried to live: brought down by a hail of bullets down Mexico way, defying a suicide bomber on a rush-hour tube or, preferably, on the job, in a threesome with two women half his age.

Funeral

It's your funeral, your last chance, an opportunity to aim one final kick at the pricks – and what better way of doing it than with the music that accompanies you into the cemetery fires or the grave? Not for you the clichéd 'My Way' or the soppy 'I Will Always Love You'. Try one of the following:

- 'Killed By Death' by Motorhead
- 'Return To Sender' by Elvis
- 'Disco Inferno (Burn Baby Burn)' by The Trammps
- 'Stayin' Alive' by The Bee Gees
- 'Going Underground' by The Jam
- *The Match Of The Day* theme
- 'Highway To Hell' by AC/DC
- 'Another One Bites The Dust' by Queen
- 'I'm Not Dead' by Pink
- The *Benny Hill* theme

Heaven or Hell

As your retrosexual soul departs from your body, you have only one more task to perform: to get past those pearly gates and into heaven itself. St Peter's going to want some details, but you've led a reasonably good life (if you don't count that weekend in Rhyl), have been good to fluffy animals and haven't bought any of Richard Dawkins' books – so you've got a pretty good chance. However, before you step into the realm of eternal ecstasy, it just might be worth checking with him: 'You do have beer on draught, don't you?'

The publishers would like to thank the following sources for their kind permission to reproduce the pictures in this book.

Getty Images: /H. V. Drees/Hulton Archive: 68; /Thurston Hopkins/Picture Post: 30
iStockphoto.com: /Gordon Dixon: 11, 60, 125
Jupiter Images: /PhotoObjects.net: 23, 78, 106
Rex Features: /Andrew Drysdale: 32, 84, 111; /Gerard Fritz: 114; /Jonathan Hordle: 41, 91; /Timo Jaakonaho: 50; /Sipa Press: 8
StockXCHNG: 20, 93, 126
Topfoto.co.uk: 94

PLATE SECTION:
Page 1: John Curtis/Rex Features; **Page 2:** Everett Collection/Rex Features; **Page 3:** Everett Collection; **Page 4:** (left) Paul Webb/Rex Features; (right) Rex Features; **Page 5:** (top & bottom) Rex Features; **Page 6:** Sipa Press/Rex Features; **Page 7:** (top) Richard Young/Rex Features; (bottom) Peter Simpson/Rex Features; **Page 8:** Time & Life Pictures/Getty Images; **Page 9:** (top) Roger Viollet Collection/Getty Images; (bottom) ©MGM/Everett Collection; **Page 10:** (top) Andrew Drysdale/ Rex Features; (bottom) Mark Campbell/Rex Features; **Page 11:** (top) Peter Cade/ Iconica/Getty Images; (bottom) Motoring Picture Library/Alamy; **Page 12:** Massimo Tonna/Rex Features; **Page 13:** Image courtesy of The Advertising Archives; **Page 14:** Topfoto.co.uk; **Page 15:** Image courtesy of The Advertising Archives; **Pages 16-17:** ITV/Rex Features; **Page 18-19:** Peter Cade/Riser/Getty Images; **Pages 20-21:** Hulton Archive/Getty Images; **Page 22:** John Selby/Rex Features; **Page 23:** Alf Wilson/Rex Features; **Page 24:** Image courtesy of The Advertising Archives; **Page 25:** Image courtesy of The Advertising Archives; **Page 26:** Lew Robertson/ StockFood Creative/Getty Images; **Page 27:** (top) M. Korach/IBL/Rex Features; (bottom) Katja Zimmermann/Taxi/Getty Images; **Page 28:** Sipa Press/Rex Feaures; **Page 29:** (top) Timo Jaakonaho/Rex Features; (bottom) Image courtesy of The Advertising Archives; **Page 30:** (top) Thomas Holton/Taxi/Getty Images; (bottom) John Powell/Rex Features; **Page 31:** (top) Isopress/Rex Features; (bottom) John Powell/Rex Features; **Page 32:** Image courtesy of The Advertising Archives.

Every effort has been made to acknowledge correctly and contact the source and/ or copyright holder of each picture and Carlton Books Limited apologises for any unintentional errors or omissions which will be corrected in future editions of the book.